FORM AND FOR

FORM AND FORESKIN

Medieval Narratives of Circumcision

A. W. STROUSE

FORDHAM UNIVERSITY PRESS

New York   2021

Visit us online at www.fordhampress.com.

Library of Congress Cataloging-in-Publication Data
available online at https://catalog.loc.gov.

Printed in the United States of America

23 22 21   5 4 3 2 1

First edition

for N.Y.C.

CONTENTS

He who would do good to another must do it in Minute Particulars.
General Good is the plea of the scoundrel, hypocrite, and flatterer;
For Art and Science cannot exist but in minutely organized Particulars,
And not in generalizing Demonstrations of the Rational Power:
The Infinite alone resides in Definite and Determinate Identity.
Establishment of Truth depends on destruction of Falsehood continually,
On Circumcision, not on Virginity, O Reasoners of Albion!
—William Blake, *Jerusalem*

INTRODUCTION

Some medieval tales grasp the foreskin as an organizing principle of style. They play with the prepuce to feel out how textual bodies may stretch, pull back, reveal, and perform a dramatic cut. If a book has a body—with a header and a footer, and a spine and index—then a textual corpus may also sometimes undergo circumcision. In *Form and Foreskin*, I explore this idea by retelling three medieval stories (stories by Saint Augustine, the poet of *Sir Gawain and the Green Knight*, and Geoffrey Chaucer).

Although I will focus here on works by three medieval Catholics, the foreskin as a literary concept has many antecedents, with analogues or roots in the ways that other traditions have talked about language. In the book of Exodus, for example, Moses shied away from public speaking because (supposedly) the prophet spoke with a lisp. When called upon to converse with the Egyptian Pharaoh, Moses lamented that he was not a great candidate for the job: Moses grumbled twice to Yahweh about what he called his "uncircumcised lips" (6:12, 6:30).[1]

Relatedly, several ancient Romans wrote manuals about how to deliver persuasive public speeches. In these schoolbooks about rhetorical style, the Roman orators commonly used the Latin word *circumcisus* to describe brief or spare speech, language whittled down to the bare minimum. For the Romans, rhetorical concision was *circum*-cision.[2]

Ideas about how to stylize the penis diverged dramatically. On the one hand, circumcision is extremely important to Jewish male identity and hence covenantal for Moses. The Greeks and the Romans, on the other hand, often condemned circumcision and may have even revered the foreskin as practically sacred.[3]

In the first century of the Common Era, the early Christians proselytized throughout the Roman Empire. They felt the influence of both of these distinct attitudes toward the foreskin. One early Christian, Saint Paul the Apostle, frequently writes about the penile top in his letters, using circumcision as a metaphor for understanding how to read God's commandments. Under Paul's influence, the foreskin became shorthand for thinking about interpretation and for marking a distinction between a text's body and its meaning. Paul's theo-poetics of circumcision—a kind of response to both

Jewish and Gentile attitudes toward the foreskin—shaped the medieval textual bodies I play with in this book.

EMBODIED METAPHORS

Paul reinterpreted the law of circumcision as an allegory rather than an actual surgery. Paul argued that true circumcision is "of the heart" (a spiritual practice performed inwardly) and not "in the letter" (a literal cut performed on the body). He conceived of the divide between the letter and the spirit in terms of circumcision, making the foreskin a synecdoche for human embodiment generally and for textual embodiment particularly.

To take a step back, let's first consider that words often seem like containers for meaning. The text-is-a-container-that-holds-meaning metaphor feeds off of the parallel assumption that the body-is-a-container-that-holds-the-soul.[4] For the textual bodies that I study here, the foreskin—a kind of container, likewise, for the male member—conceptually bridges the human body and the textual body. Text is to meaning as body is to soul . . . as foreskin is to glans. Flourishes of literary style, like a dermatological substrate, may glide between the body of letters and their soulful meaning.

My literary-theoretical *praeputium* draws meaning from Paul's theology, but implicated as well are the elemental realities of evolutionary biology and erotic experience. Spiritual, mystical, anatomical: The overdetermined foreskin is fleshly; it disappears and reappears, and connotes the slippage between body and soul, text and meaning.

FORESKIN FORMS

The foreskin's fleshiness energizes my literary-theoretical concept, so that the tissue stands as a symbol for the "letter" of textuality and especially for those elastic adornments that most appeal to our sensual appetites. Historically, Christians after Paul used the *praeputium* to describe certain literary devices. This book performs a biopsy on one particular literary structure— the allegorical narrative. To start out, though, I offer a brief survey of a few other forms that have been understood under the sign of the foreskin.

The literary preface, for instance, may have preputial connotations. Medieval wordlists (not exactly the same as modern dictionaries) would sometimes categorize the Latin noun *praeputium* ("prepuce" or "foreskin") under the verb *putare* ("to think"). Taken literally, the "foreskin," then, is a "forethought."

This etymology seems nonsensical. But the notion actually dovetails neatly with Paul's belief that circumcision "in the letter" anticipates (as a kind of allegorical premonition) a spiritual circumcision "of the heart" (Rom. 2:28). Similarly, medieval Catholics sometimes assumed that the cut of Jesus's circumcision served as a kind of preface to Christ's biography: The excised foreskin foretold the suffering of the Crucifixion.[5] A literary foreword—the text's gratuitous tip—anticipates the inner meanings that a textual body has yet to expose.

Although my book will not focus on prefaces, what you need to know, for now—and what I will dwell on, at length, later—is that medieval writers sometimes viewed the foreskin as a way of thinking about both form and time, of cutting temporality into a "fore" and "aft."

The inner/outer structure of the uncut penis—like the husk on a kernel of grain—was also useful for thinking about other doubled structures (like puns, which signify on two levels). This becomes especially true after Paul, who described circumcision as doubled (literal and figurative). As though to emphasize that point himself, Paul used wordplay in his writings on circumcision (like when Paul joked that his opponents should be "cut off": Gal. 5:12; Phil. 3:2–3). Medieval monks sometimes described witty speech as "uncircumcised."[6] Later, the poet John Donne justified his use of puns by celebrating the "holy juvenility" of Paul's writings on circumcision. One early admirer of Donne, writing an elegy for the poet immediately after his death, celebrated Donne's witty poems for being wrapped up in "the foreskin of fancy."[7] Many famous poets, besides, have written humorous poems about foreskins, even explicitly calling attention to wit and its relation to uncircumcision.[8]

Along the same vein, the literary-theoretical foreskin has also become the plaything of vicious bigots. For centuries Gentiles have charged that Jews, by practicing circumcision, thereby become spiritually calloused, insensitive to certain scriptural truths. In the sixteenth century, for example, Martin Luther argued that Jewish circumcision produced a thick, deforming epidermis. Cutting off the literal foreskin, Luther said, cuts off Jews from true spiritual perception and prevents them from properly reading the Bible.[9]

Versions of this slander have had a long life. They also circulated in the letters of Ezra Pound, a fascist who—though his stock has fallen—remains a prominently canonized poet. Pound, the editor of T. S. Eliot's *The Waste Land*, believed that he had incubated that poem inside the womb of his foreskin. From his preputial womb, Pound gave birth to the poem's textual body, and then he supposedly circumcised the poem by excising Eliot's womanly excesses (thereby making the poem modern and manly).[10] He exposed the glans of Eliot's text, he thought, in a process that he described in both anti-Semitic and misogynist terms.

Pound follows a long tradition of Christian theologians reading the *praeputium* as able to encapsulate a reinterpretation of an existing text and regarding literary appropriation as an act of "circumcision." In the fourth century, for example, Saint Gregory, bishop of Nyssa, argued that, when reading Greek philosophy, Christians must notice that these works possess a "fleshy and alien foreskin" of fallacious doctrines. Gregory argued that, in order to cite pagan sources, they first require imaginative interpretations that read out whatever feels "fleshy and uncircumcised."[11] Appropriation, with this view, demands a circumcising hermeneutics.

I have already noted that the Romans used *circumcisus* to describe speech cut short through rhetorical *abbreviatio*. Some medieval Latin Christians, borrowing this term from the classical rhetorical tradition, more explicitly linked *circumcisus* with the foreskin. One interesting tidbit: In the fourteenth century, Nicholas Love, in *The Mirror of the Blessed Life of Jesus Christ*, advised his readers to regard the Circumcision of Christ as proof that Christians must "circumcise" their speech by practicing silence or decorum. Love rendered more explicit how Christ's circumcision (in its exegetical and incarnational proportions) could give meaning to a monastic style of abbreviated speech. He even put this theory of circumcised speech into practice: He abruptly ended his chapter on the Circumcision, cutting it short.[12]

One of my favorite examples illustrates how several of these devices work all at once. In a twelfth-century sermon on the Circumcision of Christ (celebrated as an annual festival by medieval Christians), Bernard of Clairvaux used the metaphor to think about reading and writing. Bernard's homily focused on interpreting one line from Luke's Gospel, which is the only scriptural mention of Christ's circumcision: "And after eight days were accomplished, that the child should be circumcised, his name was called Jesus" (2:21). Opening his lecture, Bernard described circumcision itself as a literary act—an "abbreviation"—and he stylized his own interpretative method as a kind of circumcision. To quote the sermon's opening:

> We hear in these little words [from Luke] a large sacrament of piety expressed. We hear the whole lecture which the Lord has composed over the earth with the abbreviated Word. He had been abbreviated in the flesh, and was even more abbreviated in accepting the circumcision of the flesh. He was reduced a little lower than the angels, the Son of God, clothed in human nature; for now not spurning [to be] the remedy of human corruption, plainly [he is] indeed lower than them. We have, therefore, here, a large document of faith, and a manifest exemplum of humility.[13]

The wit of Bernard's sermon derives from the play between "big" and "small."[14] Bernard contrasted Luke's "little words" with their "large message." After divine circumcision "abbreviates" the "lecture" of the Godhead, human interpretation unpacks this concision. Interpretation then expands abbreviation into its fuller meaning, as a "large document."

Meaning shrinks, lengthens, and shrinks again. And, as Bernard repeats later on in his sermon, Luke's little line makes an "abbreviated" account of the bigger truth of the Gospels. Circumcision, figured as a textual event, makes sensible Luke's literary abbreviation and Bernard's interpretative amplification. The play between circumcised, short speech—as a placeholder for the spiritual essence of witty, long speech—makes brevity truly the "soul" of wit.

As Bernard suggests, *abbreviatio* (circumcision) is the obverse of *amplificatio* (giving flesh to interpretation through long, interpretive discourses). I take Bernard as a cue to use uncircumcision as a way to apprehend literary *amplificatio*, the process of embellishing texts by drawing them out into long narratives (often with allegorical personifications as extra adornments).[15]

As will become clear, my three texts aesthetically embody this notion. They employ narrative forms that are modeled upon the foreskin. They create doubled layers of meaning, which are to be read under the circumcising aspect of allegoresis. In other words, each possesses a narrative body that unfolds as a fleshy plot—stretching out and pulling back, and climaxing with a sharp, circumcising cut that exposes (under the tale's outer skin) the inner nut of allegorical essence.

FORETHOUGHTS AND METHODS

In a tradition that stretches from Moses to the modernists, writers have thought about language under the sign of the foreskin.[16] Much of this material now looks bizarre and, frankly, a bit hard to stomach. And at least one bigoted strand of this tradition is fouly smegmatic. Indeed, Paul's interpretation of circumcision resonates with the core metaphysical problematics of the Jewish/Christian divide or dialectic.[17] But for the most part, this book will address only a tiny sliver of the subject.

I will not delve deeply into the anti-Jewish dimension of this tradition, since smarter writers than me have already examined this topic.[18] Though I am truly tempted to suggest that debates about the foreskin may have something to do with the racialization of skin, this claim is, for now, well outside of my knowhow. Likewise, medieval texts circulated on parchment—actual skin—yet this book will not deal in manuscript studies nor even, for that matter, have much to say about wounds or violence in general. Neither does the book investigate works by women (like the twelfth-century visionary Agnes Blannebekin, who, in a divine revelation, received Christ's own Holy Prepuce to eat like a Eucharist).[19]

My choices may seem odd, especially in light of how medieval studies must contend not only with the field's characteristic exclusivity but also and relatedly with how white supremacist groups have frequently employed medieval symbolism.[20] If I seem too circumspect about these issues, I nevertheless hope to address them indirectly.

My purpose, however, is more modest than the kind of far-reaching cultural study that would adequately treat the prepuce, as a literary-theoretical construct, in its cultural, political, religious, and ethical proportions (as these pertain to questions of sex, gender, and ethnicity). My approach is more thematic than historical.[21] *Form and Foreskin* chooses one peculiar metaphor and traces that metaphor's movement in a narrow choice and number of texts.

My main concern is to complicate received scholarly wisdom, which has taught that premodern people often viewed the textual body as a *female* body. Pioneering feminist medievalists, to whom I am deeply indebted, have noted that medieval theologians sometimes understood the body of the written word as feminine (in a heterosexist fashion that constructed interpretation as a masculine act of "penetration," patriarchally trafficking in women through reading and writing).[22] To this proposition, I want to offer a queer complication. Alongside the paradigm that grasped textuality as feminine, the foreskin also codified a hermeneutics more ambivalent about heterosexism.

Perhaps counterintuitively, I find value in my minuscule scope and fractional method. I focus on the works of three canonical, presumably cisgendered, Christian male authors precisely in order to revel in how these authors relished in the foreskin as an ironizing adornment.

In opposition to the many nasty forces who conceive of a "Western Culture" as a phallic, fascistic unity—with a unique claim to Truth—I wish to advance how an apparently phallic tradition (a tradition preoccupied with penises) actually has grasped Truth not only as unitary but also as plural, and not only as eternal but also as temporal, and not only as transcendentally meaningful but also as experientially available through the messy shuttling of narrative (of plot, story, rite, process). My apparently canonical texts are, as I show, mysteriously double, slippery, elastic—enigmatically sliding from literal to figurative—*praeputia* fully available to poetry and parable and play.

This investigation, ultimately, is an experimental, maybe campy, contribution to the relatively understudied subject of medieval narratology. By narratology, I simply mean a theory of narrative. And I mean, moreover, the underlying theory of narrative that governs the ordering of story, the construction of character, and the (allegorical) interpretation of the text.[23] Here I explore how the foreskin, as a literary-theoretical idea, conditions narrative bodies and implicitly interrelates narrative bodies with broader questions of temporality and embodiment.

Form, like the foreskin, may seem trivial. But, as our fragile public life becomes increasingly diced up into opposing factions, I imagine that poetic form may actually interest readers from many positionalities. I would like to write for lay Catholics, who are immersed in a living tradition; for wicked sinners, who are irresistibly curious about the genitals; for progressive scholars, who are eager to queerly reread the past; for practicing poets, who are keen to locate offbeat sources of inspiration; and for readers of literature generally, who may simply desire a quirky perspective on some of the old classics.

Tightly circumscribed, *Form and Foreskin* may not fully satisfy scholars of medieval cultural studies, but it may appeal to anyone who loves poetry, outré readings, queer readings, and/or who is interested in homosocial conversations and in the body-as-text metaphor. Each chapter, to invite such readers, is divided into almost epigrammatic sections, so that you may feel free to skip around. And since—as I have said—medieval writers understood witticism as a foreskin, I have used a lot of *cheesy* wordplay. And since—as I have said—Roman rhetoricians understood concision as *circum*-cision, I also try to write succinctly. And since—as is likely already clear—I am a champion of stigmatized body parts, I also urge you to read the endnotes, a textual erogenous zone fully worthy of the numerous scholars in whose footsteps I follow.[24]

But of course, I cannot become all things to all men. Nor will taking a cue from Saint Paul necessarily win me many fans: I risk sounding like a heretic to those whose are devoted to Paul sincerely, and I risk sounding like a reactionary to those who, long ago, lost interest in Paul. Nevertheless, I have tried to write this book with some pep and zing because I want to make a tiny bit more space for a medievalism that is a kind of liberal art.

If I can show how a small school of poetics developed around metaphors of circumcision, maybe this will help to deheterosexualize, in some small way, the corpus.[25] This book is just the tip.

THUMBNAILS

Each of the following chapters retells a peculiar tale by a major canonical author. You could say, then, that this book is a kind of critical anthology organized around themes of circumcision and attuned to questions of narratology. You could say, further, that I am trying to identify a literary genre. Call it the *circumlogical narrative.*

In broad strokes, I would categorize a genre by its typical themes and by its typical, formal structures. In this case, I am characterizing the circumlogical narrative by its emphatic themes of circumcision and by its narrative patterns, which draw upon Paul's theology of circumcision. Foregrounding their own allegorical meanings, these tales amplify their textual bodies precisely in order to stage an unveiling of their inner, spiritual meanings. All the while, these stories revolve around cuts, nicks, and even actual foreskins. Implicitly underlying this structure—and rendered explicit by themes of circumcision—is Paul's theory that the uncircumcised "letter" contains the circumcised "spirit."

I should stress, however, that the stories in this collection are not one-to-one uses of Paul's theory. Instead, the stories that I discuss are attempts—experiments, even—by later writers to work out how Paul's attitude toward circumcision may (or may not) provide a sound model for rhetorical composition.

In my first chapter, "The Gospel According to the Foreskin," I will explicate Paul's theory and focus on Saints Peter and Paul. These Apostles argued vehemently about whether Christians needed to circumcise. Imaginatively, Paul reinterpreted circumcision under an allegorical aspect—as not a literal but a metaphorical commandment. I will detail Paul's formulation as my theoretical groundwork for thinking about narrative bodies and explain how his writings on circumcision have caused considerable debate, providing an open-ended and contested model for literary craft (and hence for the diverse narratives that I will go on to discuss). I will also read the story of Peter and the Sheet Let Down from Heaven (Acts 10:9–20, 11:2–5). This allegorical vision teaches Peter that he may befriend "uncircumcised men," wrapping up the veil of visionary allegory with the prepuce.

Also seeming to employ Paul's *praeputium* as a model for allegorical narrative, Saint Augustine tells of a boy whose abundant foreskin throws him into ecstatic trances. My second chapter, "Saint Augustine and the Boy with the Long Foreskin," illustrates how the prepuce—literal and theological—underwrites this allegorical narrativity. I examine the literary strategies that Augustine uses to relay this story in his *Literal Meaning of Genesis*, showing how a hermeneutics of circumcision shapes Augustine's style (especially his control of narrative time). But I show, as well, how the dissonances in Paul's theory led Augustine to find this vision utterly incomprehensible.

A rather more secular story—but one collected in a manuscript of religious material—the romance of *Sir Gawain and the Green Knight* takes place on the Feast of the Circumcision. In my third chapter, "Nicking Sir Gawain," I demonstrate how Pauline circumcision controls the poem's narrative trajectory (where flesh wounds mark major narrative turns and intercut scenes enflesh the narrative body). I also discuss how my interpretation may pertain to the Middle English tradition of alliterative poetry, to chivalric masculinity, and to the poem's manuscript context. This story, *Sir Gawain and the Green Knight*, is the circumlogical narrative par excellence—in my view, a classical realization of the genre.

More speculatively, I turn next to a work that less clearly thematizes circumcision. In my fourth chapter, "The Foreskin of Marriage," I treat Chaucer's Wife of Bath. As I will show, medieval theologians used Paul's theory of circumcision to theorize the sacrament of marriage, leading an early glossator to refer to the Wife as her husband's "foreskin." After I establish an interrelationship between marriage and the allegorical *praeputium*, I argue that the Wife's Tale applies a hermeneutics of circumcision to the allegorical structure of her tale's marriage plot. I suggest that the Wife vernacularizes and feminizes the Latinate *praeputium* in order to circumcise the marriage plot.

Finally, I will try to get a grip on how this medieval metaphor illuminates some contemporary controversies. I want to graft onto my textual body still more organs. This book ends with a Coda (from the Latin for "tail").

CHAPTER ONE

THE GOSPEL ACCORDING TO THE FORESKIN

And on the next day, whilst they were going on their journey, and
drawing nigh to the city, Peter went up to the higher parts of the house
to pray, about the sixth hour. And being hungry, he was desirous to
taste somewhat. And as they were preparing, there came upon him an
ecstasy of mind. And he saw the heaven opened, and a certain vessel
descending, as it were a great linen sheet let down by the four corners
from heaven to the earth: Wherein were all manner of fourfooted
beasts, and creeping things of the earth, and fowls of the air. And there
came a voice to him: Arise, Peter; kill and eat. But Peter said: Far be it
from me; for I never did eat any thing that is common and unclean.
And the voice spoke to him again the second time: That which God
hath cleansed, do not thou call common. And this was done thrice;
and presently the vessel was taken up into heaven. Now, whilst Peter
was doubting within himself, what the vision that he had seen should
mean, behold the men who were sent from Cornelius, inquiring for
Simon's house, stood at the gate. And when they had called, they asked,
if Simon, who is surnamed Peter, were lodged there. And as Peter was
thinking of the vision, the Spirit said to him: Behold three men seek
thee. Arise, therefore, get thee down and go with them, doubting nothing: for I have sent them. . . . And when Peter was come up to Jerusalem, they that were of the circumcision contended with him, saying:
Why didst thou go in to men uncircumcised, and didst eat with them?
But Peter began and declared to them the matter in order, saying: I was
in the city of Joppa praying, and I saw in an ecstasy of mind a vision . . .
a great sheet let down from heaven . . .
—Acts 10:9–20, 11:2–5

When the early Christians began to spread the Good News,
they often addressed very different audiences, who held
very different opinions about circumcision. Some Christians were themselves circumcised Jews. Or they preached

to Jews. But some Christians were Gentiles. Or they preached to Gentiles. The New Testament almost always refers to these communities with genital metonyms. In other words, the foreskin was the very mark of distinction between these groups. Saint Paul wrote, for example, "to me was committed the gospel of the uncircumcision, as to Peter was that of the circumcision" (Gal. 2:7). Paul preached, in other words, the *evangelium praeputii*, the Gospel of the Prepuce.[1]

This chapter considers how Paul's ideas about circumcision created a theoretical framework for my school of narratology. I examine Paul's writings on circumcision contextually, showing how Paul responds to Jewish and Greco-Roman attitudes toward the foreskin. And I discuss early, diverging interpretations of Paul. I suggest that the foreskin—its contradictory meanings in Paul's sources, its ambiguous meaning in Paul's letters, and its constructedness as ambivalently homoerotic—energizes the *praeputium* as a tool for conceptualizing literary style.

Then, zooming in on the story of Peter and the Sheet Let Down from Heaven (quoted in the epigraph), I propose that, in this story from the Acts of the Apostles, Paul's theory of circumcision seems already to be starting to take narratological shape in the form of an early circumlogical narrative. For a detailed roadmap of the chapter's argument, you may finish reading this section, or skip ahead, and ascend with me to Paul's Third Heaven.

First, I argue that Paul wrote in response to two distinct traditions, the Hellenistic and the Judaic, each of which had inflected the foreskin with considerable meaning.[2] Both cultures rendered the prepuce (or its lack) as a quintessential symbol of that culture's aesthetic and spiritual ideals. Paul synthesized these traditions by crafting a compromise between, on the one hand, those early Christians who advocated for circumcision and, on the other hand, those who sought to forgo the rite. By Paul's time, these traditions had already started to come together, with contemporaries like Philo of Alexandria interpreting circumcision in Greek terms (reading the ritual as an allegory and as a mode of ethical discipline). Paul's hermeneutics of circumcision built on these ideas, allegorizing circumcision and cutting off the ritual from its literal referent, with his new interpretation retaining elements of both cultures, torquing his construction of the *praeputium* with dissonance.

Next, I examine how this hermeneutics ambiguously interrelates the "spirit" and the "letter." I detail how contemporary critics as well as early

Christian disciples of Paul have disagreed about how Pauline allegoresis operates. I suggest that this critical controversy ultimately stems from the ambiguity of Paul's letters themselves.

Finally, I will retell the story from Acts, already quoted in the epigram, in which Peter beholds an allegorical vision that allows him to commune with the uncircumcised, a narrative that puts into practice the Pauline allegoresis of circumcision.

JEWISH CIRCUMCISION OF THE HEART

In Genesis—after Abram has been called by God, journeyed through Canaan, received several covenantal promises, and propagated one son through his concubine—in chapter 17, God promises Abram a son by his elderly wife, Sarai, and, in this chapter, announces the covenant of circumcision. First, "the Lord appeared to him" (Gen. 17:1). Then God tells Abram, "neither shall thy name be called any more Abram, but thou shalt be called Abraham" (Gen. 17:5). Next, God foretells his "perpetual covenant" (Gen. 17:7). And God marks Abraham genitally: "You shall circumcise the flesh of your foreskin, that it may be for a sign of the covenant between me and you" (Gen. 17:11). In this famous scene, preputiotomy seems almost to manifest a circum-visionary-linguistic complex, a conflation of circumcision with visionary experience with literary stylization.

Circumcision has to do with narrative. The single word is itself a narrative—with characters performing the act, enacting an ancient and perpetual, divine commandment.[3] And this narrative is set within the narrative of Genesis.

And circumcision resonates with prophecy. The Hebrew Bible associates penile pruning with divine visions and depicts the foreskin as a veil that prohibits spiritual understanding. Some rabbinic commentaries even codify circumcision as a prerequisite for access to knowledge of God's word— an idea that anticipates later uses of the foreskin-as-language metaphor.

Connected, perhaps, are the cutting, the renaming, and the prophetic vision of the covenantal promise. Circumcision is theo-onomastic, a rewriting of the sign into a sanctified nomen (from Abram to Abraham) that conforms to the divine order. As though posthectomy inflects language with prophecy—as though circumcision cuts time—the covenant is a promise.

And circumcision is akin to interpretation. According to some rabbinic commentators, Abraham's genital initiation allowed him to behold God.[4] Kabbalists have assumed that a circumcised penis grants access to the sacred. The medieval Kabbalist *Zohar* notes that "before Abraham was circumcised [God] spoke with him only by means of the 'vision,'" whereas "when one is circumcised one enters the name and is united to it."[5] According to the zoharic teaching, posthectomy places a man into a visual relationship with God. Circumcision, in this regard, would allow a circumcised man to understand the Bible, because circumcision exposes the concealed glans and analogously exposes the concealed meaning of the Bible's true teachings.[6] Maybe the opening opens the text.

Or, circumcision seems metaphorical. The Hebrew Bible frequently employs circumcision as a sign for spiritual insight. In Leviticus, at Sinai God explains the punishments for violations of the law, admonishing sinners for having an "uncircumcised mind" (26:41). The uncut flesh figures mental impurity, where circumcision figures true understanding. Body, soul, and text interrelate by way of circumcision. In Deuteronomy, Moses pronounces that "the Lord thy God will circumcise thy heart, and the heart of thy seed: that then mayst love the Lord thy God" (30:6). Likewise in Jeremiah, God gives the commandment to "be circumcised to the Lord, and take away the foreskins of your hearts, ye men of Juda" (4:4). The ethical-spiritual self is here imagined in phallic terms. And in Ezekiel, the prophet relays the Lord's fury that the Israelites had "brought in strangers uncircumcised in heart, and uncircumcised in flesh, to be in my sanctuary" (44:7). The metaphor— not at all a dead one—acknowledges actual amputation, emphasizing how the more abstract foreskin (of mind or heart), as a metaphor depends upon the literal foreskin.

THE PLATONIC FORM OF THE FORESKIN

In his play *Salomé*, Oscar Wilde explores the implications of the metaphor as a marker of distinct cultural sensibilities. Wilde puts into the mouth of a Jewish character the observation that Greek philosophers "are not even circumcised":

> A THIRD JEW: God is at no time hidden. He showeth Himself at all times and in everything. God is in what is evil, even as He is in what is good.

A Fourth Jew: That must not be said. It is a very dangerous doctrine. It is a doctrine that cometh from the schools at Alexandria, where men teach the philosophy of the Greeks. And the Greeks are Gentiles. They are not even circumcised.[7]

The joke, in my understanding, is that the foreskin—a Hellenistic attachment to uncut boys—is its very own ontology, incompatible with the God of Abraham.[8]

It is almost as if, to the Greeks, the prepuce embodied the very philosophical ideals of self-control and male beauty. If Greek philosophy privileged temperance, then cutting seems to have impeded this virtue. An erection, in a way, indicates that a man has lost control of his body and become possessed by sexual desire, and the Greeks seem to have associated an exposed glans with just such a state of shame.[9] By this logic, a circumcised penis looked just as unphilosophical as an erect one. A visible glans (whether bare through arousal or circumcision) outed a man as passive to his passions.[10]

The penis, in the Greek context, might be a political creature, because the Greeks practiced a fair amount of public nudity. In civil life, the Greeks regarded an exposed *tête* as vulgar nakedness. In order to avoid a preputial faux pas, competitors during the Olympic festivities—otherwise completely unclothed—would wear a string (called the *kynodesme*, or dog leash) in order to fasten their foreskins shut.[11]

The Romans, too, guarded the glans, sometimes by wearing a ring called the *fibula* (hence, "infibulation"). Nonathletes also wore such devices, indicating that the leash and the ring both functioned more symbolically than practically.[12] Plato specifically praises the sexual restraint of athletes, and the *kynodesme* symbolized a philosophical commitment to moderation. Preputial occultation realizes a Hellenistic commitment to a sound mind in a sound body. Uncircumcision muzzles the unphilosophical dog.

The Greeks used two terms for cut members—*psolos* (an adjective) and *apepsolemenos* (a participle)—both meaning "with the glans exposed." Several times, Aristophanes refers disparagingly to *psolos* men.[13] Meanwhile, the Latin *verpus* (a noun) means the erect penis, while *verpa* (an adjective) means "circumcised."[14] The close association between circumcision and arousal follows from the view that the glans is the crown of unphilosophical crudeness.

The Greeks and Romans projected engorged brutishness onto Dionysian beasts and foreign *apepsolemenoi*. Greek art employs the glans as a source of coarse humor. On vase paintings, the penis's nut appears only on images of satyrs, *apepsolemenoi* whose onion-domed pricks attest to their animality. The glans also rears its head in representations of foreign-born slaves (typically depicted as barbarously tumescent).[15]

The Romans, likewise, represented the uncouth Priapus—the god of rustic fertility and sexual assault—as comically well endowed, with his acorn showing. Yet Greek art always shows the idealized male body with a dainty member, bedecked with an exaggerated foreskin, perhaps grown long from frequent leashing (an indication of temperance).[16]

At least some of the Greeks believed that nature had designed the prepuce as a filigree in order to decorate the body. Herodotus called the foreskin "seemly."[17] Ancient anatomists described the foreskin as a protector of "decorum" and argued that nature had created the foreskin as a beautifying "ornament."[18]

If the foreskin itself is not exactly the good, the beautiful, and the true, it could embody this ethos. Socrates in the *Phaedrus* had explained that beautiful human bodies can inspire the kind of philosophizing that directs the soul back toward the Forms.[19] By extension, the beauty of the foreskin might encourage meditation on Truth. In this way, the Greeks, no less than the Jews, claimed for the *praeputium* a mystical power—but in contrary terms. The foreskin is a tool of philosophy.

But as I will explain, for Paul, Christ has so fully fulfilled the law (and its commandment to circumcise) that neither physical presence nor absence any longer have determining force; neither the sensual nor the formless necessarily matter in relation to a higher "circumcision."

ANTITHESIS AND SYNTHESIS

Greco-Roman culture abhorred Jewish circumcision. Note that Roman writers like Horace, Petronius, and Sidonius all wrote unflatteringly of Jewish circumcision.[20] And Tacitus had proposed that Jews practiced circumcision out of an innate depravity.[21] During the second century BC, the Greek king Antiochus IV may have precipitated the Maccabean Revolt by banning the practice of circumcision.[22] And under the emperor Hadrian the Jews "began a war, because they were prohibited from mutilating their genitals" (according to the *Augustan History*, an admittedly unreliable source).[23]

But Jews also assimilated to uncircumcision. Responding to Anti-ochus IV, some Hellenized Jews regrew their foreskins (1 Mac. 1:15–16). The physicians Galen and Celsus advocated for plastic surgeries, while an out-patient method (the *Iudaeus pondus*) also regenerated the lost tissue.

Just to get a sense of how this conflict might play out in literary prac-tice, take a look at this poem by the Roman poet Martial. Epigrammatist of the bathhouses, Martial mocked Jews for using the *pondus* and for wearing sheaths on their penises.[24] In this poem, Martial attacked a Jewish literary rival as "circumcised." Martial and his literary competitor crossed swords:

> That you are green with jealousy and run down my little books wherever you go, I forgive: circumcised poet, you show your sense. This too leaves me indifferent, that you plunder my poems while you carp at them: cir-cumcised poet, herein also you show your sense. What does upset me is that born in Jerusalem itself you sodomize my boy, circumcised poet. So! You deny it, you swear to me by the Temple of the Thunderer: I don't believe you. Swear, circumcised one, by Anchilaus.[25]

The poem—a self-conscious reflection upon poetic personae—links the foreskin with literary craft. The refraining appellation "circumcised poet" is applied four times throughout the poem like an incantatory taunt. Peritomy engenders intimacy between the two poets, who share not only books and verses but also a beloved ephebe.

Martial's manly mantle greases this friction, yet ultimately the two poets belong to alternate linguistic universes. The prophets saw circumcision as the shibboleth of prophetic language, but Martial jokes that circumcision inhibits civil speech. Martial brags that he—as the proud possessor of a prepuce—will certainly win in this literary-erotic contest. In other words, penile ablation marks the Gentile's antagonist as verbally foreign, so that the Roman cannot trust an oath issued by the circumcised poet. Martial suggests that, in a sense, circumcision marks the border between linguistic universes or opens up into a realm where words mean differently.

Gradually, however, Greek philosophy colonized the Jewish penis, so that ideals of circumcision came to be understood on Greco-Roman terms. Greek thinkers like Plato invented the idea that textuality resembles a body, and by the beginning of the Christian era, Hellenized Jewish thinkers sug-gested that the textual body held a soul.[26] The body/soul dualism inflected a Hellenized view of Jewish circumcision: Jews began to interpret the "body" of the law of circumcision as though it signified a higher, allegorical, spiritual content. Circumcision, thus understood, functioned as a spiritual discipline, an ascesis that regulated not only the body but also the mind.

Writing in the first century, the Hellenized Jewish philosopher Philo of Alexandria subscribed to a Middle Platonist belief that nonrational desire corrupts the soul. And for Philo, the foreskin represented the excesses of corrupting, unregulated passion.[27] Philo, throughout his commentaries on Scripture, reads circumcision as "the figure of the excision of superfluous pleasure."[28] Expounding upon the biblical injunction to "circumcise the hardness of your hearts," Philo said that circumcision means to "prune away from the ruling mind the superfluous overgrowths sown and raised by the immoderate appetites of the passions."[29] Writing also on the text of Genesis, Philo repeated the point: "Circumcision of the skin is a symbol, as if to show that it is proper to amputate off superfluous desires."[30] In other words, a Platonic tendency to allegorize led to the conclusion that circumcision enacts and represents a philosophical ideal.

By reading circumcision allegorically, Philo used the excised foreskin to unite literal and metaphorical, physical and spiritual, body and soul. When Philo provided a rationale for circumcision, he claimed that the ritual constructs a homology between the mind and the penis (which are equivalent, since both are procreative organs):

> For as both are framed to serve generation, thought being generated by the spirit force in the heart, living creatures by the reproductive organ, the earliest men held that the unseen and superior element to which the concepts of the mind owe their existence should have assimilated to it the visible and apparent, the natural parent of the things perceived by sense.[31]

For Philo, the one-to-one correspondence between mind and penis makes literal circumcision a means to accomplish spiritual circumcision. Philo argued that actual circumcision accomplishes symbolic circumcision because of the fact that "the bodily organ of generation . . . resembl[es] thought, which is the most generative force of the heart," and he suggested that the foreskin persuasively signifies the passions because of its sensual nature.[32]

Philo's allegoresis of circumcision did not fully transcend the ritual, however. That is, Philo did not take the symbol to such an extreme that he would renounce actual circumcision, keeping only its symbolic meaning.

Philo insisted, on the contrary, that the interpretation of the "inner meaning" of symbols must not neglect the outer:

> It is true that receiving circumcision does indeed portray the excision of pleasure and all passions, and the putting away of the impious conceit, under which the mind supposed that it was capable of begetting by its own power: but let us not on this account repeal the law laid down for circumcising.[33]

Philo imagined literal and symbolic circumcision as inseparable. So, Philo not only recuperated circumcision as an ideal of Greek philosophy; he also mapped the body/mind dualism onto the literal/figurative dualism—an overlap condensed upon the member, whose inner/outer layers (once disciplined) neatly produce a new poetics of the prepuce. Through his allegoresis of circumcision, Philo syncretized Jewish and Greek preputial ideals. Paul, writing around the same time as Philo, undertook the same project but took the allegoresis of circumcision one step further.

THE GOSPEL OF THE FORESKIN

The construction of language as foreskin-like, I have suggested, germinates in the Greek and Jewish traditions, perhaps even with these two cultures embodied by diverging preputial aesthetics. Along with other Hellenized Jews, who had begun to syncretize these traditions, Paul developed a reconstruction of the foreskin. In so doing, he elaborated the foreskin as a symbol of textuality.

You could say that Paul exploded the terms of the debate. Despite his mission as Apostle to the Uncut, Paul described himself as "circumcised the eighth day" (Phil. 3:5). And Paul also personally circumcised Saint Timothy (Acts 16:3). Yet Paul—opposing Peter—rejected the necessity of physical circumcision. Paul, in arguing that status is not determinative of one's identity as a Christian, proclaimed that "circumcision is nothing, and uncircumcision is nothing" (1 Cor. 7:19). Although Paul seems to have written circumstantially—addressing letters to particular audiences—he seems generally to have understood circumcision as a meaningless question.

Paul shifted the terms of the discussion by redefining circumcision. In his letter to the Romans, the Apostle develops a theory of how Christians should understand circumcision. Paul's rereading of the prepuce advances a method of reading generally, so that the foreskin becomes a key term in Christian literary theory. After Paul, the foreskin became a symbol of symbology itself. While receptions of Paul have differed wildly, Christian readers have still consistently regarded Paul's understanding of the *praeputium* as a crucial method for the interpretation of Scripture.

Paul and the other Apostles argued about whether Christians needed to undergo circumcision. This conflict nearly tore the new church apart. But Paul created a complicated, imaginative solution. He sided neither with the procircumcision nor with the anticircumcision factions, believing instead that Christians needed to undergo a spiritual kind of "circumcision."

Beyond physical circumcision, Paul prioritized a kind of universal circumcision—an excision that occurred on a higher plane, which Paul called a "circumcision of the heart." Paul put forth his radical theory of circumcision in his letter to the Romans. Although the circumstances are not entirely available, Paul seems to have composed this epistle maybe between 53 and 59 and had addressed the letter to a congregation of Roman believers in Christ (probably including at least some Jews), seemingly in preparation for a journey by Paul to Rome.[34] The second chapter deals with questions relating to the nature of the law and the righteousness of God's judgment, putting forth an influential interpretation of the law:

> For he is not a Jew, who is so outwardly: nor is that circumcision which is outwardly in the flesh. But he is a Jew that is one inwardly and the circumcision is that of the heart, in the spirit not in the letter: whose praise is not of men, but of God. (Rom. 2:28–29)

As Paul understands "circumcision," the rite is a spiritual process. Whatever the state of the body—circumcised or uncircumcised—Paul makes clear that the circumcised heart is paramount. (Note that the proposition defines circumcision as possible in at least four distinct permutations: circumcised body/uncircumcised heart, uncircumcised body/uncircumcised heart, circumcised body/circumcised heart, uncircumcised body/circumcised heart.)

What I want to draw attention to is that—even as Paul privileges the circumcision of the heart and abnegates any bodily circumcision—the chain of signifiers inevitably slips back to the foreskin as the main sign for thinking about meaning. Even if circumcision is pointless, foreskin or no, the metaphor still attaches to the foreskin. And the foreskin is universally determinative of the human heart, regardless of ethnocentric law or even sex and gender.

Paul inserted himself into a tradition of thinking with the foreskin. Clearly, Paul agreed with scriptural precedents and with his contemporary interlocutors: The Hebrew Bible had established circumcision as a symbol and as a mental and spiritual construct. And in this way, Paul is not ground-breaking. Also, contemporaries (like Philo) had understood literal circumcision as speaking to a metaphorical meaning and even enacting a spiritual discipline.[35] (Other first-century Jews also sometimes had even doubted the necessity of actual circumcision in certain, specific cases.)[36]

But, despite previous allegorizations of circumcision, Paul performed a rather more radical cut: He denied totally the significance of literal circumcision, prioritizing metaphorical and spiritual circumcision. Whereas Philo had preserved circumcision as a literal practice that provided a reference for the metaphor, and whereas Philo tended to take concrete circumcision as the basis for his readings of circumcision as a philosophically motivated practice, Paul abstracted circumcision entirely, regarding it purely as a spiritual process.[37] These are small differences, but circumcision is, perhaps, a question of small differences.[38]

Paul read the law "in the spirit not in the letter." Note that Paul's rereading of circumcision implies a hermeneutics (a way of reading). Paul's own interpretation of circumcision presupposes a method of interpretation, of deciding that the spirit and the letter may be opposed. By transposing the meaning of circumcision into a figurative dimension, Paul discerned a meaning for the body and also for the textual body (that is, the letter of the law). In eschewing outer marks upon the body, Paul eschewed the letter of the law. Paul championed the spirit and vacated the body, yet allowing that the body *may* be marked—it just doesn't matter.

This theory of exegesis uses the *praeputium* as a metaphor for conceptualizing textual layers, distinguishing between textual spirit and textual letter, and later this will become a narratological principle. But however transcended, the literal foreskin remains an important frame of reference for Paul and his readers. Paul's use of the penis to think about allegory involved, after all, a living and not a dead metaphor: Paul himself possessed a circumcised penis, and he himself had performed the ritual. In a Greco-Roman context—and, frankly, in any context wherein men possess foreskins or see them at bathhouses—Paul's readers would understand his discussion of "inner" and "outer" in relation to an intuition that the foreskin exists as an "outer" cover upon the "inner" glans. Through Paul, the flesh became word: "Circumcision" came to mean the spirit as opposed to the letter of a transvaluated *praeputium*.

RECEPTIONS OF PAUL

Paul's experience is hard to pin down. Although he had apparently beheld the Third Heaven, Paul himself, in relating this vision, did not know "whether in the body, I know not, or out of the body, I know not," (2 Cor. 12:2). No wonder, then, that Paul's theology of the body has resulted in considerable controversy. Scholars have read Paul's stance on preputiotomy in diverging ways. I want to parse out some of these interpretative questions not in order to answer them but in order to suggest that they point to a fundamental tension within Paul's sense of circumcision, a tension that has perhaps helped propel the trope's use.

Critics have not developed any consensus about the precise meaning of Pauline circumcision as it pertains to allegory. Instead, Paul's views on circumcision have generated an interpretative crux, so that Paul's allegoresis of circumcision fuels a multitude of allegorical approaches. The foreskin—an ambiguous figure—has served as a flashpoint in debates about the nature of Christian exegesis.

Postmodern thinkers have argued that Paul severed sign from referent. For these readers, Paul announced a fully allegorizing hermeneutics in which arbitrary signs point toward a transcendent meaning that denigrates the sign itself. In other words, Paul's promotion of the spirit belittles the letter—with anti-Jewish implications: The maligning of the "old" law of circumcision has justified, as well, the maligning of Judaism. Thus some readers imagine that Paul made the figures of "circumcision" and "uncircumcision" into pure symbols, cut off from the literal foreskin—a stark divide between, on the one hand, an embodied literalism and, on the other, a disincarnate spiritualism.[39] Perhaps Paul's circumcision creates a spiritualizing dualism that obliterates cultural difference in the name of universalism, but ethically, this implies an inhumane rejection of the body (with the "Jew" and "letter" marked as "body"), a spiritual universalism predicated upon vicious racism.

One further prooftext for this reading of Paul, from a discussion of the law in the letter to the Galatians:

> There is neither Jew nor Greek [i.e., no distinction between the circumcised and the uncircumcised]: there is neither bond nor free: there is neither male nor female. For you are all one in Christ Jesus. (Gal. 3:28)

Perhaps Paul abnegates all human identity. Except, of course, that Jesus Christ was a very particular human being—a strong personality with a playful sense of humor and a hot temper, who played favorites with his friends, loved his mother, and was, of course, a circumcised Jew. In other words, the very point at which humans would, in Paul's scheme, escape distinction is also the very point that returns us to the distinct human person. But I editorialize.

In any case, Paul's theory of circumcision may also structure a problematic understanding of temporality. By rereading circumcision, Paul demarcated between the "Old" and the "New," between an earlier, literal law (given to the Jews before Christ) and a later, spiritual Gospel (revealed and fulfilled to Christians after Christ). In this way, allegorical reading distinguishes between "then" and "now," so that a present, allegorical spirit has presumed to retroactively reread or supersede a previous, literal letter.[40] In other words, Paul's circumcision not only cuts between literal and figurative, but "circumcision" slashes time. This will become important later on in my book, when I discuss stories that unfold through temporal structures that are defined by circumcision.

In any case, some of Paul's early readers understood him as proposing, through circumcision, a stark dualism. In the first century, the Epistle of Barnabas employed the figure of circumcision in an anti-Semitic discussion of allegory. The Pseudo-Barnabas demarcated between pagan (literal) uncircumcision and Jewish (spiritual) uncircumcision. Citing Jeremiah 9:25, the Pseudo-Barnabas condemned Jews because they supposedly do not read allegorically. "All the heathen are uncircumcised in the foreskin," the Pseudo-Barnabas wrote, "but this people is uncircumcised in heart."[41] Thinking about allegory in terms of circumcision, the Pseudo-Barnabas set up a divide between carnal, Jewish reading and spiritual, Christian reader.

But such interpretations of Paul have not found complete acceptance.[42] Indeed, the letter to the Romans did not necessarily imply a dualistic contrast between the "spirit" and the "letter."[43] Just because Paul saw the spirit and the letter as distinct, that does not therefore mean that Paul saw the spirit and the letter as opposed.[44] Perhaps Paul did not, in fact, offer an interpretation of circumcision; instead, maybe Paul provided a new definition of circumcision's location. The notion of a "circumcision of the heart" may not entail an allegorization of fleshly circumcision. Rather, Paul may have been proposing that there is just one kind of circumcision, on the heart.[45] This is not, then, a reconfiguration or interpretation of actual circumcision but a different identification of circumcision altogether. Perhaps, then, Paul understood physical circumcision as an interpretation of spiritual circumcision and not the other way around. This reading of Paul would regard the figure of circumcision as proposing an interrelationship between spirit and letter, instead of an opposition. And it regards the spirit as informing the letter, rather than the letter embodying the spirit.[46]

And, indeed, some of Paul's early readers understood him in this way. Augustine, for example, explained in his *Confessions* that he learned about Christian allegory partly through Ambrose, who regularly repeated Paul's dictum that "the letter kills." Augustine developed a theory of allegory more in line with Paul's hermeneutics than with the theologians between the two thinkers.[47] Whereas writers like Origen and Justin had rejected Jews and Judaism outright, Augustine saw the Old Testament and the New Testament in a relation of continuity.[48] Augustine's exegetical methods allowed for a more positive assessment of Jewish law and for an understanding of the fleshly body as the natural home of the soul.[49] Augustine did not sever literal and figurative: He sees the figurative simply as the fulfillment of the literal—so that Jewish circumcision and Christian uncircumcision interrelate not dualistically but dialectically.

SPECULATION

In a moment I will read the story of Peter and the Sheet. But first let me make some conjectures. The foreskin, I want to suggest, is enigmatic and anatomically ambiguous. Where it begins and ends and whether and how it exists seem more easily defined through its excision, really, than through its actual presence. And so, the uncircumcised foreskin has an almost virtual existence (it withdraws, dissolves, disappears). As some of the loosest skin on the male body, it can figure for human embodiment—even as its ambiguity makes it useful for imagining the "spiritual" layer between the bodily and the supernatural. Perhaps this ambiguity even calls into question the penis as a sign of male gender. I might even call the foreskin "queer."[50]

More complicated still, Paul's paradoxical understanding of uncircumcision makes sensible for Christians the ambiguous, mysterious, multivalent. The foreskin shuttles between the "phallus" and "meaning," contesting a monolithic "phallologocentrism." Giving meaning to the notion of a metaphysical "foreskin of the heart," circumcision is very literally the lack upon which Paul's *praeputium* is based.

Or, let's think for a moment about the foreskin by analogy to the distinction between sex and gender. Some might hold that a biological indicator of sex (say, the penis) also correlates with one's gender identity (say, maleness), whereas some might propose a more radical break between sex and gender, with the genitals in no way indicative of one's gender identity. In a similar way, some might hold that the penis (specifically its foreskin) correlates with one's ethno-religious identity (say, Jewishness), whereas some (such as Paul) might propose a more radical break between this sex, as it were, and one's relationship with identity categories.

It is not a coincidence that the "sex" question condenses upon the genitals, for Paul would obliterate not just the Jew/Gentile distinction but also (as if coextensively) the male/female distinction. If "circumcision of the heart" aims to rewrite the circumcision/uncircumcision binary, this hermeneutics of circumcision dovetails with Paul's rereading of other identity binaries (as in, "There is neither Jew nor Gentile, neither slave nor free, nor is there male and female"; Gal. 3:28). Again, maybe Paul proposed a transcendence of identity categories altogether, yet ironically Paul's master term for theorizing this transcendence is ethnically coded and, of course, gendered, caught up in the circumcision/uncircumcision binary that it would transcend.

If phallocentric, this hermeneutics draws its power not from the penis per se but from the penis's superfluity. It could be that the foreskin is a way of sidestepping the penis, of decentering the phallus, a workaround. But then again, the *praeputium* is one mechanism by which patriarchy subsumes femininity into itself. With phallic tissue as the means to radically deconstruct binary oppositions of identity, the phallus assumes the status of the master signifier, for the phallus appropriates to itself even the power to abrogate its own binary logic. In other words, the male genitals, in assuming the prerogative to transcend those categories of identity that are constructed in relation to the male genitals, thereby command an even greater authority. Once projected into the spiritual realm and turned into an overarching symbol for all humanity (whose particular genitals, circumcised or uncircumcised, male or female, are now inconsequential), this *praeputium* serves to phallicize, though androgynously, all people. A foreskin covers or uncovers anyone's heart.[51] This is, I might argue, one temptation created by the notion of picturing God as an incarnate, circumcised man.

In later chapters, this book will explore how (after Paul) medieval writers often think of the "veil" of allegory as a prepuce. Preputial tropes, employed to describe rhetoric, attest to the capacity of the male anatomy to function as means for experiencing the plasticity and multiplicity of literary meaning.

I don't want to go too far into social psychology mode, but preoccupation with circumcision suggests a homoerotic ambivalence. Texts may thus seem to be male gendered, as though created in a patriarchal lineage whereby men create textual "foreskins" for other men to read, gloss, misread, appropriate—manipulate, cut, stretch, graft—in a literary tradition of male/male genital contact (thus Pound's wicked, mythical birthing of *The Waste Land*).[52]

Meanwhile, figures of circumcision inflect this homosociality with erotic violence. As a kind of disciplinary technology, circumcision—whatever its covenantal importance—registers male/male genital contact in terms of bloody sacrifice, at once embracing and disavowing homoerotic pleasure. Thus Pound cut apart the textual body of *The Waste Land*, cutting off its feminine excesses in order to circumcise, and masculinize, the text.[53]

As symbolic covering, uncircumcision wraps together disparate thinkers; as cutting, circumcision marks distinctions between those thinkers; and, constructed as gender-neutral or even queer, the foreskin enables procreation within a male-dominated literary culture. These metaphors of circumcision speak, also, to the anxiety of male/male literary influence.

The tension of this circumcision/uncircumcision dialectic motorizes the tradition. I have suggested that, when Abraham receives the commandment to circumcision, Genesis proposes a circum-visionary-linguistic complex. In light of Paul's more full-throated theory of circumcision-as-allegory, circumcision also becomes a structuring principle for the narratives that I will discuss in my next three chapters. But before the "tradition," I can already discern Paul's theory being put into literary practice within the New Testament, in the story about Saint Peter eating dinner with a bunch of uncircumcised men.

PETER AND THE SHEET LET DOWN FROM HEAVEN

If Paul defines allegoresis through spiritual circumcision, the story of Peter and the Sheet Let Down from Heaven implicitly operates according to Paul's theory, unfolding as a lesson in allegorical reading and with pronounced themes of circumcision. In Acts, Peter beholds a wondrous vision of a "great linen sheet," a giant veil-like film that descends from heaven loaded with unclean animals (10:11).

After Peter witnesses the sheet, he proceeds to eat dinner with "men uncircumcised" (11:3). Peter's meal with these Gentiles scandalizes the other Apostles, who ask him for an explanation. And Peter responds by rehearsing his encounter with the sheet, which he has taken as a sign that Christians can disregard kashrut and associate with the uncircumcised (11:6–18). Though the story also concerns food laws, scholars have established that the vision bears more upon the taboo of contact with Gentiles (known in the text as the "uncircumcised") than on food.[54] The story therefore pertains to the Circumcision Controversy, resolved later in the same book (Acts 15).

The Sheet Let Down from Heaven operates as an allegory: Peter reads the vision as a fabulous sign of supersession, of a new order that has reinterpreted the old law. The thematic of circumcision corroborates, as I see it, the preputiality of the amplified narrative's allegorical veil. That is, the veil of the allegory entwines with the prepuce (both the literal *praeputia* of Peter's dining companions and the *praeputium* of Pauline exegesis, which Peter's vision accomplishes through allegorical interpretation). In other words, the story narrativizes the Pauline association of the foreskin with the allegorical veil and spiritual circumcision as allegoresis. Or, it puts into narrative practice Paul's theory of circumcision.

Moreover, the sheet vision evinces how Pauline circumcision structures a particular approach to the ordering of narrative time. The story uses what narratologists might call a repeating narrative: It narrates twice an event that happened once (Peter experiences the vision once, and after the author of Acts relates this experience, as well as the Apostles' reactions, Peter retells what has happened to him).[55] I wager that Luke employs this technique in order to embody, through narrative, the circumcising allegoresis that enables Paul's mission to the Gentiles.

As cited in the epigram to this chapter, Acts 10:9–16 narrates Peter's experience of the vision, and then, in Acts 11:1–18, the narrative repeats: Peter narrates his vision again, using the same details but adding an exegetical commentary that explains how the vision answers the Apostles' concerns about the Old Law ("But Peter began and declared to them the matter in order"; Acts 11:4). Peter's narration constitutes not only a repeating narrative but also a metanarration (a narrative that is told from within the main narrative).[56]

The shift in narrative level (to a metanarrative) also entails a shift in perspective. The author of Acts had first told the story from a vantage seemingly outside of the story (an extradiegetic narration, in nerdy narratological terms). But then Peter, from inside of the narrative, recapitulates the story (an intradiegetic narration, if you want to be technical). In other words, the repetition of the story entails a transition between points of view, from a third-person narrator to an internal focalization.

By repeating in the first person, the narration accentuates how the allegorical experience promotes interiority: Peter, formerly the object of discourse, now becomes the subject of discourse, as though the vision, once understood in its allegorical aspect, has served as a switchpoint by which Peter learns the Pauline dictum: "He is a Jew, that is one inwardly; and the circumcision is that of the heart, in the spirit, not in the letter" (Rom. 29:2). Now that Peter has allegorized the law, the story exists within a new frame.

As Peter relates, his encounter with the allegorical vision transformed him from an outwardly circumcised practitioner of the Old Law into an inwardly circumcised Pauline Christian (Acts 11:5–10). Through narratological amplification, the inner content of the vision-allegory finally becomes accessible—just as, for Paul, the allegorical meaning of Scripture becomes fully realized after the Incarnation, or as the Gospels become disseminated through the Pentecost. The retrospective, intradiegetic repetition embodies this inward shift: Peter's metarepeating narrative performs, in miniature, the typological reinterpretation of history. The story puts into practice a circumlogical narratology.

Relatedly, an understanding of the human body can control the kinds of spaces into which narrative may enter.[57] Here, the sheet story evinces how a

Pauline construction of the body inflects the narratological deployment of space: The circumlogical vision, by rereading the law, enables the figure of Peter to enter into the homes of Gentiles (Acts 10:28).[58] Through the spiritual circumcision of allegoresis, Peter eschews the law of fleshly circumcision and enters into the homes of the uncircumcised. Allegory transforms Peter's bodily experience from circumcised to "circumcised." A space that had been narratologically off-limits has now become available as a setting accessible to the character and, overall, to narration.

Meanwhile, by projecting Peter into a second-degree narrative, the story formally enacts the Pauline division between spirit and letter. The metanarration adds a second layer to the narrative—and it deploys this second layer in order to retell and to interpret the events narrated by the first layer—in order to establish narratologically the spirit and the letter as distinct yet interconnected and (hierarchically) ordered. The metarepeating narration adds a layer to the narrative, creating, as it were, a "sheet" in which to envelop the story.

This thickening of the narrative body, further, motivates the forthcoming revelation. Peter's allegorical reading of the sheet, also an allegorical reading of the law, is an entry into an uncircumcised territory. The thickening—the developing of narrative layers—seems almost to facilitate the turn to allegoresis that advances a Pauline practice of spiritual circumcision. The body must stretch out in order to be cut.

If different literary genres operate according to different understandings of temporality, and if, as scholars have already suggested, Pauline typology implies a particular temporal sense, then perhaps the structure of Peter's vision crafts a particularly Pauline time-sense.[59] By thickening time through a repeating metanarrative, and by thickening space through the allegorical vision's assertion of spiritual law's involution of the material world, Acts narratologically enacts an emerging form of Pauline allegoresis.

Peter's vision emphatically combines an amplified metanarration with a repeating narrative to an exegetical end.[60] The repeating narrative reinterprets the vision, installing the typological temporality of Pauline history into the narrative framework. The repetition in Acts may also differ from the repetition that commonly occurs in the Old Testament, where repetition often happens at a rhetorical level but less often at a narrative level.[61] Joseph, of course, reveals himself to his brothers and recalls their treatment of him, and God narrates n times that he has brought the Israelites out of Egypt, and the book of Judges tells history as a cyclical pattern of errancy, punishment, and deliverance. But the narrative repetition in Peter's vision, by seeking to install Paul's hermeneutics, explicitly operates as a disavowal—or fulfillment—of such precedents, insisting upon the particularly "spiritual" method of its autointerpretation.

Insofar as the metarepeating narrative succeeds in asserting Paul's circumcised hermeneutics, the narrative's structure offers a recapitulation, in miniature, of Pauline circumcised history. By repeating the visionary experience, the story rereads the past from an allegorical perspective, precisely as Pauline circumcision rereads the Old Law.[62] The narrative structure argues for the Pauline reading practice that structures its very method of organizing time and space.

This story occurs at a pivotal moment in Acts, as the book strives to install Paul as the principal Apostle. In the book's opening chapters, Peter cites Old Testament prophecies as proof of Christ's coming, and Peter's words often cut the hearts of his listeners (e.g., 2:37, 5:33, 7:54). In other words, Peter circumcises hearts through the interpretation of Scripture. These early chapters thus prepare for Paul's appearance by depicting Peter as a practitioner of a Pauline exegetical method.[63]

Chapters 10 and 11 of Acts tell the story of the sheet as part of a project of promoting the spiritual over the fleshly. The allegorical tale leverages Peter's position among the Apostles in order to confirm the validity of spiritual visions generally and to advance Paul's vision in particular, and, thereby, the vision of the sheet promotes both Paul's approach to the question of the Law and Paul's apostleship itself. At the Council of Jerusalem—recounted in Acts 15—Paul's approach to the Law wins out over James's objection that circumcision should remain valid.

CIRCUMLOGICAL HERMENEUTICS

Paul's ideas about the *praeputium*, I have said, draw upon the allegorizations of circumcision articulated by Paul's contemporaries, even as these ideas respond to Greco-Roman attitudes toward posthectomy. The apparent contradictions within Pauline circumcision mean that, as later writers attempt to develop Paul's metaphor of circumcision into a larger conceit that explains Christian allegory, these different writers produce quite divergent theories.

Paul's distinction between the "spirit" and the "letter" of circumcision generated debate about whether this distinction necessitates an opposition between these two levels of meaning. Paul's understanding of circumcision licenses, for some of his Christian readers, modes of reading that connect the literal and the allegorical, and it licenses, for some of his other Christian readers, modes of reading that undermine the literal.[64] In both cases, metaphors of circumcision reign over the spirit and the letter.

Peter's vision, I think, puts Paul's theory into narratological practice. In Peter's vision, the vision and its explication bookend the narrative: The story begins with a kind of preface (Peter sees the sheet), then it continues through some amplification (Peter undertakes a short journey and goes to dinner), and finally it culminates in exegesis (Peter explicates his original vision through allegoresis). Through themes of circumcision, Peter's vision allegorizes the prepuce, and it preputializes allegorical narrative. The structure of this story—told through vision, narrative, explication—develops from the circumlogical hermeneutics that propose biblical history as an interpretive process of old literal law and new spiritual rereading.

By "circumlogical," I mean that such a theory of narrative follows from the allegorical method defined by Paul in terms of the *praeputium*, which uses circumcision to delineate between the literal shell and the inner allegorical kernel. I propose that medieval readers, at least in certain cases, apprehended the veil of the allegorical narrative as a "foreskin" and apprehended the process of allegoresis as a "circumcision." Peter's vision displays a story-telling strategy used in later medieval narratives, a narratology of circumcision.

Having established a framework for conceptualizing literary form through the foreskin, the remainder of this book applies and amplifies this framework as a narratology. Using the Pauline *praeputium* as a literary-theoretical heuristic, I analyze three medieval tales. For each of these tales, I develop new readings that elucidate how these works employ a hermeneutics of circumcision as a structuring principle that shapes character, plot, and narrative temporality. But I stress that, as these tales attempt to apply Paul's *praeputium* as a model for crafting narrative, they do so experimentally—and my readings, therefore, will highlight the ways that the stories themselves are narrativizing the problematics of the prepuce.

CHAPTER TWO

SAINT AUGUSTINE AND THE BOY
WITH THE LONG FORESKIN

There was also among us a boy who was in the early stages of puberty
and suffering from a severe pain in the genital organs. The doctors were
unable to diagnose the case. All they knew was that the affected glans
was hidden inside, so that even if they would remove the foreskin the
glans would not be visible but would be found only with great difficulty. . . . When the boy suffered from it . . . he would lose all sensation
and lie with his eyes open, seeing no one and remaining motionless
when someone would pinch him. After a time he would awake as if
from sleep and, no longer feeling any pain, would reveal what he had
seen. . . . He said that in all or in most of his visions he saw two per-
sons, an old man and a boy, and that they told and showed him what
he heard and saw.

—Augustine, *The Literal Meaning of Genesis*

Saint Augustine is not generally known for his stories about foreskins.[1] But even in his most famous work, *The Confessions*, Augustine prays to God: "Circumcise my physical lips and my spiritual
[lips] from all presumption and all deceit."[2] In the first-century
letters of Paul, circumcision had pointed toward multiple layers of textual
meaning. For Augustine (writing in the fifth century), circumcision stood
as a metaphor to grasp language in its "physical" and "spiritual" proportions. And given the intense eroticism of Augustinian theology, the term
also evokes the penis.[3]

The expression—"circumcise my outer and my inner lips"—borrows
from Moses's complaint. As I mentioned in my Introduction, Moses,
prophesying with a speech impediment, had griped to God about his "uncircumcised lips." For Moses, the metaphor of the foreskin, when applied to
speech, seemed to stand for the outer body of language (the gratuitous stut-
ter). Other examples from the Hebrew Bible, as I noted, advanced another
valence of circumcision (on the mind or heart), fueling Paul's understand-

ing of a primary, spiritual circumcision that transcended a mere bodily circumcision. Like Paul, Augustine made circumcision double (outer and inner), but Augustine maybe differed from Paul in giving credence to both kinds (outer *and* inner).[4]

And Augustine's expression operates at another level. Augustine, as a professor of Latin rhetoric, knew the Latin term *circumcisus* ("concise"). Augustine wittily reread the pagan term (as though under a Christian, allegorical aspect)—inflecting *circumcisus* as not only stylistic but also profoundly moral, a speech not just abbreviated by concision but also shorn of sin (both as interior intention and as outward performance).

Augustine used circumcision not only to theorize the confessional mode of writing but also to put this circumcised confession into literary practice. For Augustine, an ideal of circumcised speech was an aspiration—a desire to write—a prayer that Augustine directed to God, asking for divine aid in circumcising his text. If metaphors of circumcision structure Paul's approach to reading the Bible, then these metaphors also, here, imply an approach to writing, to the composition of narrative. And if I am able to argue nothing else, then this, at least, is my one, big claim: Circumcision is a stylistic principle.

To tease out how circumcision might influence the form of rhetorical composition, this chapter focuses on a little-known but utterly fascinating story told by Augustine about a boy with a very long foreskin. I examine the shape of this story—its narratological ordering, its understanding of temporality, its layers of meaning, and how Augustine unpacks these layers.

Before approaching the story, I will briefly sketch out some background, both as the story relates to Augustine's larger corpus and as it relates to Augustine's monastic vocation. Then, my retelling of the story will spell out how this tale, with its thematics of circumcision, unfolds through a circumlogical structure—a narrative patterning that realizes the "outer" and "inner" layers of its own textual body, as these layers map onto or resemble the letter and spirit of the *praeputium*. I will also consider how the *praeputium* allows Augustine's narrative to enter into a different time signature—how the supersession of "old," literal circumcision by "new," spiritual circumcision underwrites the way that Augustine relates the story in time. Finally, I will consider how and why Augustine finds this story so perplexing: As I argued in my previous chapter, the Pauline theory of the *praeputium* leads to considerable interpretative controversy, and this confusion vexes the body of Augustine's narrative, so that Augustine—even as Paul seems to be his theoretical model—effectively cannot cut into the tale's significance.

CONTEXT

After Paul, the problem of distinguishing between the letter and the spirit remained something of an open question. In our own time, questions of reading and applying Scripture still affect public life. And the definition of the "literal" is not at all settled. Like, *literally*.

For Augustine and his contemporaries, interpreting the Old Testament was a matter of major consequence and the subject of intense controversy. Augustine argued heatedly with the Manicheans, who rejected the Old Testament altogether. In several of his works, Augustine attempted to clarify a Christian approach to reading the Hebrew Bible (theorizing, meanwhile, a Christian identity in relation to Judaism). Part of this project included Augustine's several commentaries on the Book of Genesis: Augustine wrote two commentaries on Genesis and also produced scattered references to Genesis throughout his works, including an extensive commentary on Creation in *The Confessions*.

The story of the Boy with the Long Foreskin is an anecdote, really: It is based upon an incident that Augustine seems to have witnessed, probably within his monastic community.[5] But Augustine records the story within one of his commentaries on Genesis (*De Genesi ad litteram libri duodecim*, or *The Literal Meaning of Genesis in Twelve Books*). This commentary exhaustively investigates every line in the Creation stories (chapters 1 through 3 inclusive). How the foreskin relates to Genesis is a peculiar digression that illustrates the story's greater importance for Augustine's thinking (and maybe for Creation).

In the twelfth book of *The Literal Meaning of Genesis*, after he has treated every line of his text, Augustine begins to question the nature of Eden or Paradise (since the Creation story takes place there). In order to define Paradise (as represented by Genesis), Augustine turns to Saint Paul.

I said that Paul had beheld the Third Heaven. But Paul experienced this vision ambiguously: "Whether in the body, I know not, or out of the body, I know not." Augustine, in attempting to define where the Fall of Man took place, explores how Paul could not clarify how he had experienced Paradise.

Paul's confusion about the corporeal and the spiritual prompts Augustine to reflect upon the differences between the letter and the spirit of textuality. These differences are important not only to the question at hand—what is Genesis saying about Paradise—but they are also embedded in Augustine's own project of producing a commentary on Genesis (a project that requires having a sense of what the text says in letter and spirit). Paul's experience of Paradise, then, is practically and theoretically important to Augustine's project.

Paul's apparent confusion about the spirit and the body became, for Augustine, an opportunity to conceptualize the "letter" and the "spirit." Augustine considers how these terms may apply to the interpretation of texts and to the interpretation of dreams and visions (specifically mentioning Paul's vision of Paradise as well as Peter's vision of the Sheet Let Down from Heaven). By parsing out these example texts, Augustine defined the "spirit" and the "letter," and Augustine also identified what he called textuality's "intellectual" layer.

Without dwelling too much on this system, let me explain that, for Augustine, the "letter" encompasses the words that we read, the "spirit" encompasses the images that those words inspire in the reader, and the "intellectual" encompasses a true interpretation of the text. Whereas some readers of Paul had mapped "literal" and "figurative" onto "letter" and "spirit," Augustine's system harmonizes the distinction between "literal" and "figurative": Both coexist at the level of the "intellectual." (Students of Augustine may see this as a habit of Augustine's neo-Platonist mind, like when Augustine argued in the *Confessions* that, before God had created Creation—with its distinct and divisible forms—God must have first created a "nothing-something," an indistinct and shapeless form.)

Augustine arrives at what looks like a cogent, precise theory, and his three terms might be used to categorize most any text, vision, or dream. But Augustine admits to many anomalous cases that generate interpretative confusion. In fact, Augustine (always playing the modesty topos) claims to write more as "one who discusses and investigates than as one who knows." Regarding certain visions, "I confess my ignorance," Augustine says.[6]

For Augustine, the Boy with the Long Foreskin is such a befuddling case. This story is an example of a narrative that draws meaning from Paul's literary theory of the *praeputium*, but the story remains fully caught up in a messy divide between spirit and letter—caught in the confusion of "whether in the body I know not"—where the meaning of "circumcision" is not clear-cut.

My reading, below, will closely examine how, in narrating the tale, Augustine's word choice connects the state of the boy's penis with the very process of narration, so that the preputial body emblematizes the body of the narrative. My reading will also track how, in viewing the foreskin as the cause of the boy's visions, Augustine's narration further connects the prepuce with the body of specifically allegorical narrative. And I will process Augustine's control of narrative time, showing how the supersession of old, fleshly circumcision by new, spiritual circumcision directly structures the narrative's temporality.

But the tale takes a surprising twist: It comes to a satisfying, neat conclusion (as a series of events) but fails to produce a compelling, clear interpretation (as an allegorical vision). The ambiguities of Paul's *praeputium* emphatically vex the narrative. Augustine uses the *praeputium* as a heuristic for understanding interpretation and as a tool for organizing narrative. But the spiritualized foreskin still cleaves problematically to the actual, literal foreskin, in ways that open up opportunities for creative narrative development.

THE BOY

Augustine reports on a boy "with a prepuce that hung immoderately in length."[7] This foreskin brings the boy—and, indirectly, Augustine and his community—into direct and disturbing contact with the supernatural. As Augustine explains, the boy's uncircumcision throws him into fits. Doctors come to investigate, reminding Augustine's readers that the foreskin not only acts as a profound symbol for both Jews and Christians but is also, first and foremost, an actual, physical tissue, one under the disciplinary purview of physicians and anatomists.

The doctors, Augustine says, cannot treat the boy, and his prepuce is so long that it circumvents their attempt to expose his glans and find the root cause of his ailment:

> The best physicians by no means could tell what it was, except that the glans itself was hidden inside, such that, even if the prepuce were cut back—for it hung immoderately in length—still it would not have appeared but would have been difficult to find.

Here, Augustine gets up close and personal. Of course, Augustine is widely known as a very erotic writer and hot theologian. But rarely—even in discussing his own sexual exploits—does Augustine provide graphic details. While the foreskin seems not to cause the boy's actual problems—indeed, he also discharges a "stinging liquid"—still, the foreskin takes pride of place as the physical item most clearly illustrated. (Augustine adds the seemingly gratuitous detail "for it hung immoderately in length.")

No doubt, Augustine highlights the foreskin here because of its biblical subtext. Not just a few millimeters of skin, the foreskin is a profound theological symbol and fully worth narrativizing. And narrativize it Augustine does, as he relates (and subjects to our own gaze) how the foreskin hides the boy's glans. The doctors cannot assess the boy—*doctors*, plural! Apparently, the foreskin hides the glans, so that the hidden state of the *corona glandis* seems to signify the limits of human knowledge. The prepuce, covering the glans, is a veil that inhibits access to truth (maybe especially for pagan-adjacent natural scientists). Confronted with an inscrutable mystery, Gentile thinking is of no use.

The ambiguities of the boy's visions, which I will discuss in a moment, may be linked with how this particular foreskin hangs at a length that is "immoderate" (*immoderata*). This word is significant for Augustine. The "immoderate" is often upsetting for Augustine because it is a condition of ambiguity. For example, elsewhere in *The Literal Meaning of Genesis*, Augustine writes that measurement, as an abstract principle, moderates the created world.[8] The idea of moderation, then, is what holds physical bodies together and keeps worldly actions ordered and comprehensible. Moderation, as an ontological ordering, applies, as well, to the ethical life: Augustine frequently describes lust as a problem of moderation (for example, in *The Literal Meaning of Genesis* and in *The Confessions*).[9]

The boy's foreskin is so weirdly the subject of rubbernecked fascination because it is not properly bounded, ordered, measureable. It hangs immoderately in every sense (ethical, sexual, and metaphysical). And note: This notion of immoderation will influence, later, how I describe the foreskin's relationship with temporality (and the measurable boundaries of human time as Augustine plays with them in the narrative).

In any case, as Augustine goes on to relate, the boy's penis grants him a special, visionary faculty that exceeds secular knowledge (that is, that goes well beyond the ignorant doctors). The boy's preputial condition sends him into trances. He experiences heavenly visions:

Waking up after a while, now no longer suffering, he would reveal what he had seen. Then a few days would pass and he would suffer the same thing again. In all or in nearly all of his visions, he said that he saw two people, one of advanced age and the other a boy, by whom those things were told to him, or demonstrated, those things which he said that he saw or heard.[10]

The boy beholds an old man and a boy. With no great stretch of the imagination, these two people clearly signify the Old and the New Laws. Indeed, these two dispensations are traditionally personified with such figures. Where the symbol of circumcision divides, for Paul, the Old and the New—and demarcates, relatedly, the new, allegorical positions of letter and spirit—the boy's immoderately long foreskin becomes precisely the mechanism for facilitating a visionary space that pictures, in allegorical terms, the trajectory of Christian history from "old" to "new."

The vision—or, at least, the message relayed by guides—seems unequivocal and not open to many conflicting interpretations. In Augustine's own terms, the "intellectual" meaning of this vision might be that the figures relate allegorically the story of salvation. Didactically, the two guides explain to the boy how souls are saved or damned:

> One day he saw a choir of the faithful bathed in a wonderful light as they sang hymns of joy, and at that same time a company of the wicked surrounded with darkness and suffering various kinds of bitter torments. The old man and the boy were his guides, pointing out and explaining what the one group had done to merit their happiness and the other to merit their misery.[11]

Although Augustine does not transcribe, in direct discourse, the speeches of the two visionary figures, their messages seem clear enough, with the elements of the vision signifying (almost in a one-to-one representation) some of the major elements of Christian belief.

The history of human salvation is, itself, circumlogical. As Augustine spells out in *The City of God*, the literal rite of circumcision may be understood as a metaphor for the process of human history. The coming of Christ had "cut off" the foreskin of the past:

> For what else does circumcision signify but the renewal of nature by the sloughing off of old age? . . . For what is that which is called the old

covenant but the veiled form of the new? And what else is that which is called the new but the unveiling of the old?[12]

The Old Testament is conceived, here, as a foreskin that hides the New. Circumcision is the exposure of this New. In a sense, the timeline of history looks like a penis, alternately concealing or revealing its essential meaning. Circumcision figures a process of allegoresis whereby meaning is unveiled. The Old Testament, as the "concealment" of the New, is a preputial veil that must be cut off in order to reveal the truth. But the Old Testament has empowered these very terms, so that the "cutting off" feeds back into reenergizing the basis of the metaphor, if you see what I mean. The past is prepuce.

Perhaps the analogy follows from the biological fact that—especially in cases like the boy—the uncut penis appears to contain within it some mysterious kernel. The constitution of the uncut member provides a model for allegorical interpretation, a means for experiencing the "covering" and "revealing" of history. As Augustine said elsewhere, the foreskin is always ready at hand as a useful metaphor.[13]

But theologically, the analogy follows from the Pauline supposition that literal circumcision must be "cut off" interpretatively, superseded by spiritual circumcision. The shape of circumlogical hermeneutics provides, as well, a way to apprehend the structure of history in terms of the penis's hood.

Case in point: The boy's visionary guides actually prescribe that he live out, upon his own body, the trajectory of history. The two figures—old and young—tell the boy first to be circumcised (like the old law) and then to be baptized (like the new law):

> He had this vision on Easter Sunday, after spending the whole of Lent without feeling any of the pain from which he had before enjoyed scarcely even a respite of three days at a time. At the beginning of Lent he had had a vision of these two, who had promised him that for forty days he would feel no pain. Then they gave him a kind of medical prescription, advising that his foreskin be removed. He followed the advice and for a long time experienced no pain. But when his old trouble returned and he began to see the same visions, he was further advised by them to wade into the sea up to his thighs and, after remaining there for a time, to come out. They assured him that from then on he would never again experience the

bitter pain he had been suffering but only the annoyance of the viscous liquid that we have mentioned above.

The boy (as though he himself were an allegorical figure) lives out the transition from the "old" (sacramentalized as circumcision) to the "new" (sacramentalized as baptism in the sea). Yet curiously, even when the apparent cause of his visions (the foreskin) is removed, the condition still haunts and inspires yet further visions until it is finally excised through the baptism. It is as if, like a phantom limb, the foreskin needs yet to be spiritually circumcised.

Note that the boy's pains are called "his old trouble." Circumcision is, again, a "stripping off of the old." His foreskin, in needing to be cut, signifies the "old" law, but this foreskin becomes, as well, the vehicle for advancing a "new" allegoresis. The foreskin is intimately wrapped up—both as literal tissue and as theological symbol—in the convoluted way that Christian history appropriates the letter of circumcision to charge up its supposed spiritual circumcision.

Augustine saw salvation as operating both in the scope of history and in the life of the individual, a conversion (at both levels) of turning from literal to figurative.[14] The boy individually experiences the circumcision with which salvation history climaxes, an allegory caused by his body (the malignant foreskin) and acted out upon his body (the circumcision and bathing cure), with allegoresis determining the meaning of that body, and the meaning of the genitals, and the meaning of the text of scriptural history.

INVENTION

Augustine's own story-telling techniques suggest a connection between the story itself (about a foreskin) and a theory of narrative (grounded in Paul's *praeputium*). This story, I said, belongs to Augustine's larger discussion about the nature of interpretation. And the story itself is highly concerned with narration. In fact, several narrations take place, and on multiple levels. Level 1: Augustine narrates how the boy had experienced visions. Level 2: Within that overarching narration, the boy had also narrated those visions to his community. Level 3: Within those visions, two figures had, in turn, narrated to the boy the meaning of the images that he had beheld. (You can see why this might be important for thinking about Chaucer, whom I'll get to later in the book.) The boy would "reveal what he had seen," sharing how the figures "told and showed him what he heard and saw." The multiple frames call to mind the metanarration of Peter and the Sheet Let Down from Heaven, and the frames draw attention to vision and narration as the object of Augustine's inquiry.

Moreover, Augustine uses a vocabulary that echoes Latin theories of rhetorical construction. The first sentence indicates that the boy's visionary experience begins at puberty's beginning (*in exordio*). This term, *exordium*, has multiple meanings and may refer sometimes to the world's creation by God, a city's construction by its founders, or a text's introduction by its author (the common thread apparently being that all of these actions imply an agent's willful attempt at inaugurating something new). I want to foreground that the story is introduced, here, at the introduction of the boy's puberty—that the beginning of the narrative's development is coextensive with the beginning of his genital development. Or, the language of *exordium* calls attention to the foreskin as a rhetorical technique of introducing the "new."

Soon, the doctors cannot find (*inventus*) the boy's glans. The term, again, echoes Latin theories of rhetorical construction. Classically, the process of "invention" refers to the rhetorician's procedure of "inventing" persuasive arguments (the fundamental program of rhetoric). If, as I suggested, the hidden glans speaks to a certain kind of hermeneutic occlusion—an inability for the doctors to unpeel the phallus of truth—Augustine's vocabulary points to this incompetence as a problem of rhetoric, an inability to "invent."

Although Augustine does not seem to develop this vocabulary into a full conceit, the two terms subtly envelop the narrative within narration itself (even as the story is being examined—like the penis is being examined—by Augustine in order to analyze how revelation, generally, works). In this way the text constructs a parallel between the body of visionary narrative and the body of the Boy with the Long Foreskin.

CIRCUMCISING TIME

Meditating longer on "old" and "new," let me turn again to the question of time and examine how Augustine stylistically controls the temporality of the narrative. Paying attention to the story's temporality may tease out the ways that a Pauline reading of circumcision structures narrative time.

In my reading, this narrative stylizes time first through a temporal dis-tention—a stretching out of narrative time—and then through a superses-sion—a cutting off of narrative time. Effectively, Augustine pulls and cuts the preputial body of allegorical narrative—as I will explicate by recapping the story and tending to its time schemes.

Augustine relates how the boy's penile condition causes him great pains, but between spasms he loses his senses and, as if catatonic, experiences vi-sions that the boy retells upon waking up. In explaining this set of symp-toms, Augustine uses many temporal deictics (words that specify a temporal location, like "before" or "now"). Temporal markers chart the chronology of the boy's bodily pains and their visionary correlates, as these proceed in linear time:

> The acute pain would not last long; but **when** the boy suffered from it, he would shout violently and toss about like a madman. . . . And **then in the midst** of his cries he would lose all sensation and lie with his eyes open. . . . **After a time** he would awake as if from sleep and . . . would reveal what he had seen. **Then after a few days** he would go through the same experience.[15]

An apparently cyclical pattern ("he would go through the same experi-ence"), the boy's condition plays out, in Augustine's narration, as a series of events that are ordered in linear time ("when . . . and then . . . after a time") and that are experienced in measurements of time ("would not last long," "after a time," "then after a few days"). The point that I want to punctuate, right now, is that Augustine organizes this portion of his narra-tion linearly. But next, Augustine discusses the actual visions in a different time scheme.

Although Augustine had outlined his medical report by using many past-tense verbs, he now describes the visions primarily with present parti-ciples. If that sounds pedantic, look closely at the passage:

> One day he saw a choir of the faithful **singing** hymns of joy, **bathing** in a wonderful light. . . . The old man and the boy were his guides, **point-ing out** and **explaining** what the one group had done to merit their happiness.[16]

The heavenly visions are occurring in the continuous present of the parti-ciple, happening now, as if projecting the text into the eternal. Where Augustine initially had stylized the temporality of the narrative as a linear and chronological process, he now stylistically works to lend the allegorical vision a sense of infinity.

Fans of Augustine will have already pieced together how the "singing" in this vision relates to Augustine's philosophy of time. Famously, Augustine thought about time in terms of singing. In the *Confessions*, Augustine suggested that, although humans are embedded in time (living in past, present, and future), we can nevertheless experience something similar to eternity (a continuous "now" that holds together all of time) chiefly when we are singing (specifically because singing a hymn draws upon the memory, which holds together all at once the entire song in its beginning, middle, and end).

Much as Paul spiritualized circumcision, Augustine spiritualized time. Augustine conceptualized time as incorporeal (what Augustine called a *distentio animi*, or "distention of the soul"). Where circumcision is on the heart (not the penis), time is in the soul (not in the sun, moon, or stars). In *The Literal Meaning of Genesis*—actually, in the chapter immediately previous to Augustine's discussion of the boy—Augustine also used singing as an example for theorizing how humans distend the soul to apprehend time (rather than sensing with our bodies).[17] The boy's vision—narrated through the continuous present of participles—exists in this eternal, singing now, which transcends the body (specifically because the boy has lost all bodily sensation, even when he is pinched). In narrating these events, Augustine's control of verbal time illustrates how visionary space creates access to a lyrical eternity.

This spiritualization of time has implications for narrative. Classically, narratives operate through the ordering of story by beginning, middle, and end. A distention of the soul, however, may give greater credence to other orderings of story (like, for example, the repetition in the story of the Sheet Let Down from Heaven, where one event in the story occurs twice in the narrative). Here in Augustine's narrative, entry into lyrical eternity—facilitated by the visionary foreskin—abruptly restructures the story's temporality. In the next part of the narrative—after describing the boy's visions—Augustine relates the subsequent events out of their chronological sequence.[18]

Reading this passage again, note the temporal distortion that happens as Augustine relates the events of Easter before the previous events that had already occurred at Lent:

He had this vision on Easter Sunday, after spending the whole of Lent without feeling any pain from which he had before enjoyed scarcely even a respite of three days at a time. At the beginning of Lent he had had a vision of these two, who had promised that for forty days he would feel no pain.[19]

Quite in contrast to the narrative's linear introduction, and also in contrast to the liturgical calendar, Augustine places Easter before Lent. The vision, propelled by the foreskin, opened access to a transcendental, eternal "now," through which the narrative enters into a new narrative temporality that is no longer linear.

This new narrative temporality is supersessionary. That is, the narrative reordering of events would play up the supersessionary logic of Christian allegorical history. In Augustine's ordering of the narrative, Easter precedes Lent, as if to frame the boy's circumcision (at Lent) as merely the *backstory* for his superseding baptism (at Easter). Paul's *praeputium* exemplifies a historical process of "cutting off" the "old man" of Jewish circumcision in order to expose Christian, spiritual circumcision, so that history becomes a retrospective reinterpretation of the past (through transcendent allegory) rather than a purely linear process.

In this same way, the Old Testament becomes the setup for the new: The hermeneutics of circumcision, with its supersessionary typology— which rereads the Hebrew Bible (with the synecdoche of the law of circumcision) as an allegory for the Bible (with the synecdoche of the spirit of circumcision)—takes narratological form through this temporal distortion. These distortions play out upon the *praeputium* itself, whose *exordium*, amplification, and amputation enable Augustine's *inventio* and whose supersession through allegoresis should render the events susceptible to Augustine's exegesis.

Or another way to put this: If Paul's rereading of the law inaugurates a Christian temporality, then this temporality becomes philosophically formalized in Augustine's discussion of temporal distention, and this temporality structures Augustine's own circumcising allegorical narrative. The events narrated—circumcision and baptism—take place on the boy's penis, which is not just a literal tissue but also a trope of typological history. The fleshly foreskin is the pretext for an exit from bodily time into a spiritual realm of allegory and distention, so that the circumcising hermeneutic of allegory enables Christian history to play out upon the boy's body. In its linear opening, the story stretches out, and in its climactic cut, the story undertakes a circumcision of time.

"I CONFESS MY IGNORANCE"

But in a way, the boy's experience is at once too literal and too spiritual. It is as if an allegorical reading of the visions would reduce the boy to ideology, a dehumanized bearer of meaning that is supplied through retrospective allegoresis.[20] The visions seem not only to transmit, as allegory, the truth about salvation but also to transmit, as "a kind of medical prescription," the truth about the boy's sickness. For, as Augustine explains, the procedure heals him: "Never again was he carried out of his senses . . . nor did he have any of the visions he used to have . . . in the midst of his pains and terrifying cries."[21] However much truth is contained in the story, Augustine catalogues the boy's visions among the ambiguous type, which may or may not point toward truth.

The vision and/or Augustine's narration of it seem clearly to relate allegorically to Christian history through preputial figures. And the foreskin, in Augustine's story, is a sign that points to a transcendent referent—it is a symbol of visionary power and of biblical history—and that foreskin itself is encased within a narrative whose overall allegorical structure (its use of literal and spiritual layers) is predicated upon Pauline exegetical philosophy in all of its circumlogical proportions. In other words, the story recapitulates the Pauline question of "circumcision" as a mechanism for exploring how language relates to meaning both within the narrative itself and in the narrative's overall, allegorical anatomy. This circle confirms the equivalence between prepuce and allegorical veil.

Whereas Paul wished to evacuate from actual circumcision as a determining theological force, the boy's experience positions the actual foreskin as allegory. The spirit cleaves to the flesh. Indeed, the tissue is a part of—or apart from—the normative Christian body. Cut or uncut, it signs as a fleshy reminder of the letter of the law, through which the spirit takes meaning. If, for Paul, "circumcision is nothing and uncircumcision is nothing," the boy reveals how a Pauline understanding of allegory remains rooted in the actual prepuce. Foreskin and fiction are conflated, so that the two stand as signs and symbols, either of the other.

As Christians promoted allegory—the "new"—they opposed spiritual reading to literal interpretation by defining spiritual circumcision against literal circumcision. But this continually thinks in terms of the literal foreskin, which is figuratively cut off in order to effect allegoresis. To "circumcise" the "literal" foreskin "spiritually" is a dissonant concept. Augustine's story about the boy reenacts the Jewish-Christian exegetical conflict through the biography of someone who is very really circumcised. The story realizes the literal foreskin as the skeleton key to allegory, attesting to how the Christian spiritual imagination depends, still, upon circumcision. And thus Augustine himself is ambivalent about the story, not entirely sure whether it is a moral vision.

The problem is expounded further in Augustine's *Tractatus adversus Iudaeos* ("Treatise against the Jews"). There, Augustine explained that Christians no longer perform literal circumcision because "we are circumcised by putting off the old man and not in despoiling our natural body."[22] Augustine imagined reading in terms of cutting the body, even as he explicitly said that Christians do *not* cut the body. This makes sense, precisely as the terms are understood in their Pauline valence, but the double rereading requires a mental cut. The old ritual, once repressed, returns in the symbolic realm.

Christians who do not cut their bodies still "cut" spiritually, exiling the "old man" who symbolizes, first of all, the Old Testament and who relatedly stands for the injunction to circumcise literally. Christian allegoresis means circumcising circumcision, cutting off those who literally cut off the foreskin. In the *Treatise*, Augustine articulates this hermeneutic approach through personification allegory (the "old man"), so that the Jewish body epitomizes the fleshly literalism cut off by exegetical *praeputium*. This maneuver transvalues literal circumcision as a symbolic foreskin, as though to complete the break that would follow from a transcendentalizing allegoresis of circumcision.

Significantly, in the story of the Boy with the Long Foreskin, it is an "old man" and a "young boy" who appear to this *young boy* in his visions. Were this visionary able to adequately interpret his visions, he might see the "old man" and "young boy" as emblematic of the "old" and "new" laws. He might even thereby become the "young boy" of the New Testament. But the layers of letter and spirit, reality and vision seem stuck to one another, referring back to each other, almost in an endless loop without transcendent space for realizing a useful interpretation—a botched allegoresis.

No partition, indeed, can fully occur between circumcision and "circumcision," since the circumcised Jewish body remains an integral vehicle for the theorization of spiritual circumcision.[23]

"HE DID NOT REMAIN STEADFAST IN HIS PURSUIT OF SANCTITY"

After the boy receives his baptismal prescription, his visions cease, but shortly after, he seems to leave Augustine's monastic community.[24] Perhaps Augustine dodges the problems raised by his own literalism when he cuts the boy out of the story. The preputial visionary departs from the scene—as if to relieve Augustine of the challenges that the boy poses as the literal embodiment of allegorical history. Narratologically, the character is made to exit the space within which the narrative had taken place.

It is as if he has disappeared into the cut made by spiritual circumcision.

After the foreskin allows entry into allegorical space, the visionary's body evaporates, leaving behind only the ambiguous truth of allegorical fable. The boy's exit from the monastic community exemplifies precisely how this allegorical tale plays out the contradictions of the ideal of Pauline circumcision. The boy lives out the *praeputium* upon his own body, yet—having thus embodied the experience of circumcised allegoresis—he himself is transcended, his self jettisoned from the narrative. All that remains of him is an abstracted, negated "sanctity"—a disembodied circumcision—that he himself cannot experience.

If tropes of circumcision helped Paul create a sense of Christian identity, then this story seems to use the foreskin also to narrativize the boundaries of the monastic community. In trying to use the story to discern who will or will not pursue sanctity, Augustine suggests that the story has to do not only with how actual circumcision configures the boy's body but with how spiritual circumcision configures the corporate body of vowed religious. The ambiguity of the story gives narrative flesh to the ways that Pauline circumcision vexes the monastic body.

If Augustine uses the boy's body to theorize the morphology of narrative, he also uses the boy to theorize the embodied nature of the human condition. The story relates how, within a monastic context, allegoresis determines the meaning of the body and, specifically, of the male genitals. Augustine saw salvation as operating both at the level of history and at the

level of the individual, so that he understood personal conversion as a matter of turning from the literal to the spiritual. In a graphically physical way,
the boy lives out the spiritual circumcision that characterizes Augustinian
temporality. The boy's literal foreskin generates a vision of Christian history, and, with circumcision and allegory condensed upon his body, the boy
undergoes the kind of spiritual circumcision that all monks seek.

As Augustine taught, monastic rules may discipline the outer habit of the
body in order to discipline the inner will. This is as good as saying, then,
that circumcising the "outer lips" may indeed rearrange the "inner lips."
Ultimately, the letter is not dispensable, but it contributes to or even orders
the transcendent spirit (maybe as the discipline of monastic habit trains
the interior will). Circumcision begins as a bodily question but becomes
transposed by Paul onto the spirit, and this discourse would project spiritual circumcision back upon the flesh as a code for regulating the self. The
foreskin is the prison of the body.[25]

The boy's leave-taking marks, too, another kind of cut in Augustine's *The
Literal Meaning of Genesis*. After indexing several different visionary stories,
of which the tale of the boy is the final item, Augustine proceeds to explain
how such visions should be interpreted. The boy's departure, then, facili-
tates a shift from narrative to interpretation. Augustine switches personas,
taking off his storyteller's cap and donning his critical theorist's hood. Now
Augustine explains that visions like this one are similar to dreams.

In *The Literal Meaning of Genesis*, Augustine explains that some dreams
predict the future: They may present the future obscurely and figuratively,
or they may foretell events openly. Augustine notes, too, that interpretation
is quite difficult for inexperienced men, who must seek the help of more
knowledgeable teachers. Augustine's theoretical exposition, directly following the story of the Boy with the Long Foreskin, evokes the previous scene.
Like the boy's long foreskin that obscured his glans from the physicians,
allegorical dream visions hide meaning under a veil.

The story seems vexed by an inability to perceive the truth within the
skin but also by an inability to perceive the skin within the truth. It is almost
as if the prepuce, here—unbounded but bounded by the flesh—is a "nothing something." By this phrase, I mean to refer to Augustine's discussion
in the *Confessions* (in comments on Genesis) when Augustine confronts
the unbounded boundary—the formless substrate that grounds all forms—
that must have been (Augustine believed) created before Creation. For

Augustine, this "nothing something" is what gives intellectual sense to the world, though, in his imagination, it looks hideous, terrifying, confusing—a genderless womb.[26]

To conceptualize time and eternity through circumcision is to be caught up in a spirituality that sticks to the genital flesh. The Boy with the Long Foreskin illustrates the tensions within this paradigm by pruriently depicting the phimosis of an adolescent boy, by staging a same-sex probing of the boy's foreskin, by graphically translating the episode into a narration by a male author, and by performing the ritualistic initiation of teenage circumcision. I wager that the story illuminates, as well, a certain, latent pederastic dimension in Paul's hermeneutics—an interest in the "young boy" that alludes to what John Donne had called Paul's "holy juvenility."[27]

CHAPTER THREE
NICKING SIR GAWAIN

The grene kny3t vpon ground graypely hym dresses;
A little lut with þe hede, þe lere he discouerez;
His longe louelych lokkez he layd ouer his croun,
Let þe naked nec to þe note schewe.
Gauan gripped to his ax and gederes hit on hy3t;
Þe kay fot on þe folde he before sette,
Let hit doun ly3tly ly3t on þe naked,
Þat þe bit of þe broun stel bot on þe grounde.
Þe fayre hede fro þe halce hit to þe erþe,
Þat fele hit foyned with her fete þere hit forth roled;
Þe blod brayd fro þe body, þat blykked on þe grene.
And nawþer faltered ne fel þe freke neuer þe helder
Bot styþly he start forth vpon styf schonkes
And runyschly he ra3t out þereas renkkez stoden,
La3t to his lufly hed and lyft vp sone,
And syþen bo3ez to his blonk, þe brydel he cachchez,
Steppez into stel-bawe and strydez alofte,
And his hede by þe here and in his honed haldez;
And as sadly þe segge hym in his sadel sette
As non vnhap had hym ailed, þa3 hedlez nowe
    In stedde.
    He brayed his bluk aboute,
    Þat vgly bodi þat bledde.
    Moni on of hym had doute,
    Bi þat his resounz were redde.

(The green knight promptly takes his stand; with his head bent a little, uncovers his flesh; he laid his beautiful long locks over his crown, let the bare neck show in readiness. Gawain gripped his axe and heaves it up on high; setting his left foot on the ground in front, he let it come down quickly on the bare flesh, so that the man's sharp blade sundered the bones and sank through the fair flesh and severed it in two, so that the blade of burnished steel bit into the ground. The fair head fell from the neck to the ground, so that many kicked it with their feet where it rolled forward; the blood spurted from the body, shining on the green. And the [green knight] neither faltered nor fell any the more for that but strongly leapt forward on firm legs and roughly reached out where men were standing, seized his comely head and lifted it up immediately, and then goes to his horse, catches the bridle, steps into the stirrup and mounts, and holds his head in his hand by the hair; and the knight seated himself in his saddle as firmly as though no misfortune had troubled him, though no headless there. He twisted his trunk around, that ugly body that bled. Many a one was frightened of him by the time he had finished speaking.)

Sir Gawain and the Green Knight, ll. 417–43

Exit the well-endowed adolescent, and enter another young man who needs to be cut: Sir Gawain. If you already know the fourteenth-century poem *Sir Gawain and the Green Knight*, then please feel free to skip ahead (or, hang out for a sec, since the story is so worth retelling).[1]

PLOT SUMMARY

Well, it begins on New Year's Day in Camelot, when (before the feast can begin) King Arthur also wants to hear a story. All of a sudden, a Green Knight appears, dressed all in green, and (here's where it gets freaky) actually green himself! Doubting that Arthur's courtiers are nearly as brave as they claim, the Green Knight offers a challenge: Anybody can offer him a blow. But, one year hence, the Green Knight will return the blow to whoever has struck him. Sir Gawain, thinking that he's very clever, hacks off the Green Knight's head (assuming that this will end the contest once and for all). The Green Knight, however, simply grabs up his bloody head and tells Gawain, "See ya next year!" End scene. Then, about a year later, Gawain rides off from Camelot, not too thrilled that he must now meet this magical Green Knight and receive a sword blow from fantastic creature (whom, after all, Gawain has tried to murder). For a brief, Christmas repose, Gawain chillaxes at the Castle of Bertilak, whose lord also wants to play a kinky game of exchanges. Every day when Bertilak hunts, he gives Gawain the game that he bags, and, in return, Gawain must give Bertilak his winnings (kisses that Gawain receives from Bertilak's seductive wife). Later, Bertilak's wife gives Gawain a green girdle, which is apparently magical and will protect Gawain from sword blows. Gawain—always scheming—does not give the girdle to Bertilak (thus breaking his vow). On New Year's Day (one year from the poem's starting point, if you're thinking about time in a linear way), Gawain journeys away from the castle and finds the Green Knight, who, it turns out, was Bertilak the whole time—and Bertilak knows about the green girdle. Bertilak mercifully nicks Gawain on the neck and sends him home, where he feels deeply ashamed for breaking his vow. Notably, this romance exists in only one manuscript (Cotton Nero A.x), which otherwise contains not romantic but religious poetry (written, as well, in an alliterative style).

OVERVIEW

Already, you will have noted that the poem turns on two significant cuts (the decapitation of the Green Knight and the nick of Sir Gawain). And let me also call your attention to how these cuts take place on New Year's Day, which is the Feast of the Circumcision—the eighth day of Christ's life, when the infant underwent circumcision. Two major plot turns, performed as cuts, echo this liturgical Circumcision.

My reading of *SGGK* makes the methodological assumption—not uncommon in *Gawain* studies—that the poem's content mimics the poem's form, that human bodies in the poem speak to the physical experience of the poem itself.[2] In my discussion of *SGGK*, I explore how the poem frames male/female relationships and male/male relationships within a narratology underwritten by a hermeneutics of circumcision. In reading the poem's textual body, I argue that *SGGK* formally puts into practice the conceptual metaphor that grasped textuality in terms of the prepuce.[3]

My contention is that *SGGK* often imagines maleness as pliable, cuttable, and contradictory and that, according to that understanding, the poet of *SGGK* often genders the form of the romance as male (as, similarly, pliable, cuttable, and contradictory). The body of the poem, in my reading, mimics a male body, one whose meaning becomes apparent through cutting. Linked to the Feast of the Circumcision, the events of the poem explore the relationship between appearance and essence—between Gawain's social reputation as a chivalrous knight and his cynical, conflicted interior—so that the poem's major "cuts" stage hermeneutic circumcisions. The poem, then, partakes of a circumlogical narratology—similar to what I elaborated in my earlier discussions but more clearly pronounced and with a clearer sense of how "letter" and "spirit" control narrative.

I will further suggest that, although the poem theorizes its textual body as male, the protagonist's journey coincides with a feminizing of this body and that the climax of the poem circumcises this body—disciplines the male hero, disciplines the body of chivalric romances, and exposes the poem's allegorical kernel. The translation of Paul's hermeneutic *praeputium* into a romantic register advances a poetics of spiritual circumcision that ver-nacularizes this tradition. In so doing, *SGGK* attempts to conform chivalric romance with the more religiously didactic material of the rest of Cotton Nero A.x and, also, to discipline the lay male body.[4]

In the first section of this chapter, I argue for reading the form of *SGGK* through a hermeneutics of circumcision. I show how the poem alludes to circumcision and how these allusions implicitly theorize the poem's form in relation to Pauline circumcision.

In the second section of this chapter, I undertake a thorough reading of the poem's structure. I track how, over the course of the narrative, the poem's body undergoes a process of circumcision. Specifically, I see the poem's two major cuts as staging two kinds of hermeneutic circumcision. First, the initial decapitation of the Green Knight stages a circumcision "in the letter" (an aggressively literalizing, legalistic cut). Then, the poem's textual body thickens—it engages in narratological strategies of temporal distention, chiastic narration, and wit—so that the poem's textual body be-comes, as it were, fleshy and uncircumcised. Meanwhile, the poem's female figures challenge the gendering of the textual body as male and, as part of this thickening, feminize the textual body. This process motivates the final, spiritual circumcision that occurs at the poem's climax, when the nick on Gawain's neck reveals—like a circumcised allegoresis—the typological duality of the poem's main characters (each of whom exist in two distinct inflections) as well as the multivalence of the poem's own textual body. In a nutshell, the process plays out thus: a cut in the letter, a stretching out, a cut in the spirit.

In my third section, I lay out what I see as the major implications of this reading (both for understanding the poem and for my understanding of alliterative poetry). I argue that *SGGK* undertakes a kind of *translatio praeputii*—a translation of the Pauline *praeputium* into a vernacular register. By applying a theological literary theory to the genre of the romance, the poem spiritualizes this genre, circumcising romance. Through this maneuver, the chivalric themes of *SGGK*, read allegorically, accord more clearly with the more moralistic poems in the rest of the manuscript (especially *Cleanness*, a poem that, at least in part, pegs its own exploration of the literal and the spiritual to the Feast of the Circumcision).

THE POETIC BODY AS PREPUCE

In *SGGK*, themes of circumcision flag how the Pauline theology of circumcision informs the poem's solution to narratological questions. I will develop this argument in several stages. First, I will show how the poem constructs its textual body as masculine. Second, I will show how the poem, by fashioning characters and situations that signify multivalently, constructs this masculine textual body as multivalent, ambiguous, and doubled (so that it resembles the patristic *praeputium*, which signifies both carnally and spiritually). Third, I will show how the poem condenses this doubleness upon the Feast of the Circumcision—an event that, doubled, occurs twice in the poem.

The Circumcision, as I show, prompts the poem's exploration of ambiguity—and thus situates the poem's ambiguities within the frame of circumcision. Fourth, I will explain how the poem performs two cuts upon the bodies of its male characters (namely, the Green Knight and Sir Gawain) specifically in order to code these cuts as hermeneutic acts that metacritically comment upon how the poem itself invites multiple interpretations of its textual body. These two cuts, in their metacritical vectors, theorize Paul's distinction between literal and spiritual circumcision. The gratuitous decapitation of the Green Knight, as I will argue, stages a carnal reading of the (male, textual) body. In contrast, the merciful nick upon Gawain's neck stages a spiritual reading of the (male, textual) body—a reading undertaken both upon the character of Gawain and upon the poem.

In this climactic scene, when Gawain is symbolically circumcised, he reads Old Testament figures. And he sees them as analogues for his particular situation. This performs an autobiographical exegesis, a spiritual reading of Scripture that becomes crucial to Gawain's new, "cut" sense of self, uncovering his true character beneath its fleshly shell. Meanwhile, the poem's own doubled meanings become explicit at exactly this moment.

THE POEM'S MASCULINE TEXTUAL BODY

The poem obsesses over male bodies and beastly bodies, as well as over the physicality of feasts and forests, bedrooms and castles. Just as much as the body of Lady Bertilak, these various bodies structure the poem's language and indicate the physical experience of its sounds and rhythms. The feminization of the poem's textual body marks a critical turn in the story, and I will address this later. For now, I will explain how, in its opening passage, the poem fairly explicitly constructs textuality as masculine.

At its outset, the poem identifies its textual body as masculine. The intricately ornamented bodies of *SGGK* blazon an intricately ornamented structure—an alliance of form and content that undergirds the poem's exploration of male honor codes.[5] *SGGK* illustrates all kinds of bodies (male and female, animal and botanical, architectural and natural, culinary and vestimentary). By employing these bodies, the poem explores various ways for expressing the physical experience of its poetry. Predominantly, the exposition of *SGGK* renders this poetic body as a human male, and, like the bodies of the poem's characters, the poem's body undergoes drastic transformations.

These transformations act upon a poetic body initially established as masculine, as in the first fitt, where the second strophe describes the poem's own language as manly. Promising to retell the story faithfully, the poet figures the craft of poetry as virile:

> As hit is stad and stoken
> In stori stif and stronge
> With lel letteres loken
> In londe so hatz ben longe.

(The form in which it is set down and fixed, in a brave and powerful chronicle enshrined in true syllables, is that in which it has long existed; ll. 33–36)

The description of the poem's story as "stif and stronge" echoes descriptions both of the poem's male characters and of their exploits. The "stori stif

and stronge" resembles the body of Arthur, called a "stif kyng" who stands
"stif in stalle" (ll. 104, 107). The story also resembles the body of the Green
Knight, twice called a "stif mon." And it resembles the body of Bertilak,
later called "stif" (ll. 322, 332, 846). The Green Knight holds a "stif staf," and
he engages in a game of "stif" strokes with Gawain (ll. 214, 287, 294). Likewise, Lady Bertilak will call Gawain "stif," and the poem refers to Gawain
twice as a "stif mon" (ll. 1496, 570, 2369). This phrase, "stif mon," occurs
four times in *SGGK*—a collocation all the more significant for its lack of
alliteration. The poet uses the phrase not arbitrarily to meet formal require-
ments but because of a conventional assumption about masculinity. From
the first fitt, the poem establishes its text as mimicking characteristics of the
male body.[6] The description "stif and stronge" ascribes macho characteristics to the poem.

The poem's textual body also mimics the loyalty of knightly chivalry. The
"lel" letters "loken" together "in londe." These alliterative links resemble the
knightly virtue of faithfulness ("lel," or loyalty).[7] The letters practice chivalric loyalty. Later in the poem, Lady Bertilak will call into question both
loyalty and its relationship with textuality. In fitt 3, Lady Bertilak insists
upon the basic correspondence between textuality and courtly love when
she explains to Gawain that romances uphold "þe lel layk of luf, þe lettrure
of armes" ("the faithful practice of love, the very doctrine of knighthood";
l. 1513). Lady Bertilak further explains that "Hit is þe tytelet token and tyxt
of her werkkez / How ledez for her lele luf hor lyuez han auntered" ("It is the
rubric written at the head of their words, and the very words themselves,
how men have risked their lives for their true love"; ll. 1515–16).

Asserting that "lel luf" constitutes the "lettrure," "title," and "text" of romance, Lady Bertilak discerns a commonality between textuality and the
romantic relationship that she will try to leverage against male bonds. Lady
Bertilak appeals archly to loyal love, convincing Gawain to hide the girdle
from Bertilak out of "loyalty" ("bot to lelly layne fro hir lorde," "but faithfully to conceal it from her lord"; l. 1863). Bertilak and Gawain advance a
male-male ethics of loyalty by using the word "lelly" to describe Bertilak's
promise to hide Gawain's shame (ll. 2124, 2128; see also l. 2366).

With these events yet to come, the "lel letteres" of the first fitt establish
the poetic body as belonging to a masculine covenant (leaving open, for
now, whether such letters lock together as a man to another man or as a
man to a woman).

The story circulates "in londe" and belongs to the same ancient genealogy that built the poem's setting. *Sir Gawain*'s opening stanza recounts the Trojan diaspora and the colonization of Britain. Occluding women, the stanza's foundation myth envisions civilization as the prerogative of male egos:

> Ticius to Tuskan and teldes bigynnes,
> Langaberde in Lumbardie lyftes vp homes,
> And fer ouer þe French flod Felix Brutus
> On mony bonkkes ful brode Bretayn he settez . . .

(Ticius goes to Tuscany and founds dwellings, Langaberde raises up homes in Lombardy, and far over the French sea, Felix Brutus founds Britain with joy on many broad slopes; ll. 11–14)

With loyally locking letters, alliteration binds men to their lands and to their deeds. Strong and stiff and loyally locked, the letters resemble male heroes (like Achilles and Patroclus, whose hearts, as Lydgate says, "were lokkid"; 3.70). The formal fusion of phonic repetition embodies the drives of the male heroes. The poem, joining the alliterative tradition, joins a patrimonial poetic history.[8]

THE DOUBLENESS OF THE MASCULINE TEXTUAL BODY

Although the poem constructs its textual body as masculine, the poem does not therefore promote a view of masculinity as monolithic or univocal. As I said, the notion of male "loyalty" may refer to either heterosexual or homosocial bonds. Moreover, the poem's protagonist becomes exemplary only as Gawain comes to acknowledge his failures. In the same spirit, the poem explores how its textual body might mimic the ambiguities of maleness. In this section, I will examine how the poem defines masculinity as inherently contradictory, and later I will explain how these contradictions inflect the body of the poem's form.

If, as I have suggested, the poem initially correlates its alliterative bonding with patrilineal ancestry, the poem also explicitly voices concerns about how contradictions typify this masculine genealogy. The first stanza describes the "tricherie" of Odysseus as "þe trewest on erthe" ("treachery, the most authentic example on earth"; l. 2). Counterintuitively, destruction leads to creation. After the fall of Troy, Aeneas founds Rome, and then

Roman heroes bring Roman civilization to Britain (ll. 1–15). The particular land of Britain undergoes changes in such rapid succession that opposing conditions become unified to the point of paradox:

Where werre and wrake and wonder
Bi syþez hatz wont þerinne
And oft boþe blysse and blunder
Ful skete hatz skyfted synne.

(Where war and vengeance and marvel have continued there from time to time, and often both joy and strife have quickly alternated ever since; ll. 16–19)

Britain encompasses contradictory states, so that paradoxical oppositions belong to a patrilineal history. As the second stanza relates, men "built" and "bred" in Britain and thereby fostered a society full of fighting: "Ande quen þis Bretayn watz bigged bi þis burn ryche,/Bolde bredden þerinne, baret þat lofden" ("And when this Britain was founded by this noble man, bold men flourished there, who loved battle"; ll. 20–21).[9] Destructive male bonds shape this history.

From the very first stanza of *SGGK*, the poet describes manhood as fundamentally compromised. The poem frankly accepts the impossibility of a complete identity, and it therefore never tries to craft a persuasive vision of straight masculinity.[10] *SGGK* does not propose a monolithic straight gender, but, from its very first lines, the poem presupposes the frailty of men and of their creations. With humans understood as inherently and deeply flawed, the poet foregrounds male vices, and he genders *SGGK*'s poetic body as male. And—as I will argue a bit later—the poet employs a poetics of circumcision in order to redeem this failed masculinity. For now, let me make some further observations on how the poem formally embodies its view of masculinity.

The stanzaic structure provides a poetic representation of a tragic maleness. In the first strophe, as I said, the poem describes the sudden turns of male-authored history, and then the stanza itself undertakes a sudden turn. It narrates the genealogy of Britain, and its concluding wheel (cited previously) offers a commentary about the nature of history as full of "werre and wrake and wonder." The shift from strophe to wheel marks a shift from narration to commentary. In its sudden change of form, the poetic body mim-

ics the poem's claims about history's vicissitudes: Just as male-authored history quickly turns, the poem itself changes course (its own body changes).
Having formally mimicked the swift changes of history in this first stanza,
the poet encourages the expectation that the form will continue to embody
the swift turns that typify manly acts of conquest, civilization building, destruction, and sin.

And other stanzas reinforce the expectation. The second strophe, for instance, celebrates the adventures of Arthur, and, as noted previously, the
strophe climaxes with a wheel that—as though providing a commentary on
the preceding—devises textuality as masculine. The third stanza describes
the court of Camelot in ideal terms but then collapses into a wheel that,
again, uses the form to stress the instability of civilization: "Hit were now
gret nye to neuen / So hardy a here on hille" ("it would be difficult to name
so bold a warrior-band on a castle-mound"; ll. 58–59).

The poem, again, aligns with a male body in most of the first fitt's other
stanzas, where detailed images of male bodies become representative of the
form. A portrait of Arthur almost completely fills out one stanza (ll. 85–
106). And four entire stanzas describe the marvelous body of the Green
Knight, while a fifth stanza represents the court's apprehension of this body
(ll. 130–231, 231–51). In quantitative terms, this amplified description of the
Green Knight constitutes 25 percent of the entire fitt (120 lines out of 490),
so that male bodies become the fitt's main means of giving content to its
form. After the lengthy description of the Green Knight, the next fitt similarly will dwell at length upon Gawain's physicality. These amplifications
run contrary to convention: The *Gawain*-Poet received few models for long
descriptions of male bodies, since majorly influential rhetorical manuals
tended to only provide models for descriptions of women.[11] Some manuals
even asserted that poets should respect male modesty by giving only scant
descriptions of the male body.[12]

SGGK explicitly theorizes its aesthetics when the poem dwells upon the
Green Knight's physical presence, from "his lyndes and his lymes so longe
and so grete" to his "bak" and his "brest" ("his loins and his limbs so long
and so big"; ll. 139, 143). Detailing how individual parts of the Green Knight's
attire relate to the whole ensemble, the poet notes that "alle his fetures
folwande in forme that he hade" ("every part of him matching completely";
l. 145). The line announces a stylistic manifesto, as the male figure becomes
a vehicle for thinking about an aesthetic principle of formal unity.

Throughout *SGGK*, individual poetic features follow the general form, and the poem manifests within itself its own occasion and reception. The poem, for example, contrives Arthur's request for entertainment as a performative utterance: "This hanselle hatz Arthur of auentures on fyrst," the poem explains, "in ȝonge ȝer, for he ȝerned ȝelping to here" ("Arthur has received this gift of strange happenings in the beginning of the young year because he yearned to hear valiant boasting"; ll. 491–92).[13] Likewise, the poem reflects upon the courtly audience of the "hanselle" ("gift"), and thereby the poem performatively installs the poem's reception within its own frame (ll. 231–51, 479–80). Through mise-en-abyme, the opening fitt's game of male aggression strives, too, to reflect the poem's own shape. The features and forms of the Green Knight metacritically reflect this aesthetic.

The Green Knight becomes, I think, a kind of personification of the poem's body. Many lines detail richly arrayed garments, embroidered and ornamented (ll. 160–70). In lines decorated by alliteration, the poem dwells upon the magnificently adorned body of the Green Knight. And when the Green Knight, decapitated, jumps back into his saddle "as non unhap had hym ayled" ("as though no misfortune had troubled him") the Green Knight becomes, as it were, a metaphor for the stanzaic structure, which, like the Green Knight, disintegrates and reassembles (l. 438). The wheels dismember each strophe, and they attach each strophe to the next. The Green Knight's grotesque body becomes a way to theorize the poem's textual body. More specifically, the cut upon the Green Knight's neck—taking place, as it does, on the Feast of the Circumcision—represents one mode of circumcising the *praeputium* of textuality (suggesting, in a Pauline way, that some kinds of circumcision have no bearing upon the spirit of the text, that the text can be decapitated yet still live).

I will later discuss how the poem's macrostructure pertains to circumcision. For now, I want to observe that the poem's stanzaic structure duplicates in miniature the occasion of the Circumcision. This poem deals in butchered bodies (from the decapitated Green Knight, to the nicked Gawain, as well as the three skinned beasts). Repeatedly, the stanzaic structure of *SGGK* cuts apart and reanimates the body of the text. In each strophe, alliterating long lines collapse into rhyming short lines—so that the poem continually dissects itself and reassembles.

Arguably, the poem fuses two poetic traditions that each serve distinct masculine ideals (one prefers the epic hero, the other the chivalric knight).

Consonants—strong and harsh and pugnacious—repeat in bands of alliterating lines. These lines often meditate statically upon settings, objects, and bodies. The wheel, however, relies upon rhyme, which unites harsh consonants with sonorous vowels in dynamic couplets that generate much of the poem's narrative momentum. Deflating from alliterative tumescence to petite lyricism, the stanza hinges upon the bob.[14] In this way, the wheels provide a kind of condensed version of the story that the alliterative lines dilate: The structure is a continual shuttling between abbreviation and amplification, of rhetorical circumcision and uncircumcision.[15] Typographically and metrically, the bob cuts the poetic body.

But I am getting a bit ahead of myself. In the next, brief section, I will further develop my proposal that the poem's macro body resembles the *praeputium* by examining how the poem correlates its doublings with the occasion of the Circumcision. Then, I will return to the cutting of the Green Knight in order to consider how this cut stages an allegoresis.

DOUBLENESS AND THE FEAST OF THE CIRCUMCISION

Circumcision invites a double reading, since the rite signifies, for Paul, both in the letter and in the spirit. As I will discuss, the Feast of the Circumcision serves as the occasion, in *SGGK*, for a certain narratological doubleness, and the Circumcision serves, too, as the subtext for the poem's deployment of a circumcising hermeneutics. The holiday games—and the story itself—participate in the ways that the Circumcision is a translation of letter into spirit, a liturgical performance of multivalent meaning.

As I mentioned earlier, some medieval dictionaries had categorized the *praeputium* as derived from *putare* ("to think"). This peculiar etymology assumes, with Paul, that the letter foreshadows the spirit (that the Jewish law of circumcision is a premonition of the Christian spiritual circumcision). Under an allegorizing aspect, circumcision signifies doubly. This proposition supported the gradual development of an understanding of the Circumcision as integral to salvation history.

Saint Ambrose provided the terms for crafting this reading of the Circumcision when, in the fourth century, he argued that the Circumcision marks the first occasion upon which Christ had shed his blood for humanity. In a letter written entirely on the question of why Christians need not circumcise, Ambrose dilates upon the usual interpretation of literal circumcision as a premonition of spiritual circumcision, contributing to this discourse a Christological dimension. Ambrose asserted that the law of circumcision is not only allegorical but is specifically an allegorical prefiguration of the Crucifixion, arguing that "in the blood of Christ the circumcision of all has been solemnized," thus establishing a typological equivalent between the bloodletting of circumcision and the Passion; he further wrote that "it was fitting for this partial circumcision [of the flesh] to take place before the coming of Him who was to circumcise the whole man," and, again, the "circumcision of many [through the commandment] first had to take place, because the circumcision of the Lord's passion was to follow."[16]

This formulation licenses an interpretation of Christ's Circumcision both as a confirmation of the Incarnation and as premonition of the Passion.[17] As I briefly discussed in my introduction, a homily by Bernard had announced the Circumcision both as exegetical cut and as the very realization of the Word-Made-Flesh. That is, the cutting of Christ's body in the Circumcision, for Bernard, seems to exemplify the exegetical stakes of the Incarnation, since the Circumcision realizes an abbreviation of the Word. The point is to say that the Circumcision is intimately involved in the allegorical structure of Christian salvation history: It is not merely a cut but a fulfillment of allegory and in itself an allegory, the moment when the letter of the law of circumcision realizes its spiritual potential as the harbinger of the spiritual Circumcision of Christ's incarnate, fleshly life.

The Circumcision of Christ, then, is double in the way that the exegetical *praeputium* is double: Paul reads literal circumcision in typological terms, as an allegory for spiritual circumcision. This allegorical method allows Ambrose, too, to allegorize the Circumcision as a foreshadowing of the Crucifixion. Meanwhile, allegorical reading also understands the Circumcision as the fulfillment of Old Testament prophecy. Insofar as the liturgy situates the Circumcision within the octave of Christmas, the Circumcision occurs within the range of the Incarnation biographically, even as it exists as a sign of the Crucifixion typologically. Along these lines, Christ's Circumcision was said to fulfill the Law and to anticipate the ultimate supersessionary act of the Passion and Resurrection.[18] Christ's own Circumcision acted as a kind of "forward" (that is, a covenant and/or "foreword") to the rest of his biography.

The blood of the Circumcision is a preliminary ritual, a literal bloodletting that announces, prophetically, a more spiritual purification—a translation of letter into spirit. In this way, the first antiphon for Laudes for the Feast of the Circumcision describes the Feast as an exchange: "O admirabile commercium" ("O admirable exchange"), the recapitulation of the deity into the creature's body.[19] As part of the Christmas season, the Circumcision realizes the Incarnational transmission of the Word into Flesh, as well as the exchange of Christ's blood for the blood of humanity. And throughout the Middle Ages and into the early modern period, Latinate hymnists and English poets have written such lyrics on the Circumcision in which the holiday—and its customary gift giving—represents an exchange of the literal for the spiritual.[20]

A particularly witty, vernacular example may help demonstrate the point. The seventeenth-century English poet Robert Herrick, writing "To His Saviour: The New Year's Gift," praises the Holy Prepuce as a device for officiating the Nativity's salvific exchange between God and humanity:

> That little pretty bleeding part
>   Of foreskin send to me :
> And I'll return a bleeding heart,
>   For New-Year's gift to Thee.
> Rich is the gem that Thou did'st send,
>   Mine's faulty too and small;
> But yet this gift Thou wilt commend
>   Because I send Thee all.[21]

Herrick plays upon the gift-giving delights of the holiday, exchanging his circumcised heart for the circumcised flesh of the bleeding Christ.

Even apart from the Christological dimensions of the holiday—even apart, that is, from the exegetical inflections of the Circumcision as the fulfillment of the Old law with the New spirit—the holiday is a translation. Especially in the *Acta Sanctorum*, medieval theologians had dwelt upon the pagan history of this holiday and its usurpation by Christianity.[22] In other words, the Feast is not just a supersession of Judaism but also a supersession of the pagans.

And more mundanely, the day is a bridge between old and new. The date is, of course, a liminal zone between the old year and the new year. For the Romans, the holiday had been Janus-faced.[23] And there is, then, a certain wittiness to the liturgical calendar, where the Circumcision holds together the exegetical complexities of sacred time—the supersession of the Jewish law, the syncretism with the pagan, the cut of eternity into time with the In-carnation, and the premonition of the coming Passion—with these bound up, too, in the more secular, perhaps, but no less mysterious aspect of the date itself as a curious boundary.

At the beginning of *SGGK*, these themes play out as the holiday, so con-vivial, offers amusements that create doubles. The holiday invites knights to "lede lif for lyf" ("lay life against life"; l. 98). Such games produce sets of equivalences that gesture toward the typological nature of the holiday (the exchange of literal for figurative). Notably, *SGGK* operates through doubled structures. The poem operates through a narratology informed by circum-logical typology; its interest in doubles and in doubleness communes with the holiday's concern for the translation of literal into spiritual.

Like the Circumcision itself, the poem concerns several sets of doubled characters (the Gawain of reputation and Gawain himself; Bertilak, who is the Green Knight; the Loathly Lady, who is Morgan le Fay). In addition to the doubling of these characters, the poem also structurally creates multiple levels of meaning. *SGGK* encloses the Temptation within the Exchange of Winnings and within the Beheading Game in order to develop mutually dependent plots—a structure that encourages the reader to produce initial interpretations and then to revise them.[24] For example, Gawain's approach to the Green Chapel initially appears as the conclusion of the Beheading Game, but later it becomes a postmortem on his behavior in the Castle of Bertilak.[25] And, relatedly, the poem engages both romantic and realistic modes of story telling, producing a world seemingly real and unreal.[26]

The poem's many ambiguities relate to its rhetorical occasion, New Year's Day, with ambivalence arising from the traditional sense that the New Year, a liminal moment, embraces beginnings as well as endings: Indeed, the Green Knight suggests Janus "with double berd."[27] By situating charac-ter and plot—in their doubled aspects—within the doubled setting of the Circumcision, the poem develops a poetics of circumcision, understood through Paul as similarly double (literal and/or spiritual).

In its opening fitt, the poem links its ambiguities to circumcision by in-sinuating the doubleness of the Feast of the Circumcision. The poem uses a pronounced repetition when first mentioning the holiday: "Wyle Nw Yer was so yep that hit was new cummen" ("While New Year was so young that it was newly arrived"; l. 60).[28] Here, the doubling of the "new" New Year corresponds with the holiday meal, described in the next line: "That day doubble on the dece was the douth served" ("that day the company on the dais were served double [portions of food]"; l. 61). The line implies something "double" about the "new" New Year. The Circumcision is "that day doubble," that is both old and new, uniting both.

The Green Knight proposes just such an exchange—a game that involves the doubling of one blow for another. After the Knight and Gawain have sworn their pact, the Green Knight asserts that they must "refourme we oure forwardes" ("restate our terms"; l. 378). They "rehearse" again "al the covenaunt" (ll. 392–93). The word "covenant" connotes Abraham's covenant with God, as does "forward."[29] Wittily in *SGGK*, on the Feast of the Circumcision, these same words refer to cuts.

As lyrics on the Circumcision attest, Christ undertook his literal circumcision in an exchange with the Old Law that produced spiritual circumcision, and, in a roughly analogous way, the Green Knight will exchange his decapitation for the spiritually renewing nick upon Gawain's neck. The story's doubled cuts hinge upon the Circumcision, and their exchange draws upon the Circumcision's traditional position as the volta upon which Christian typology turns. This process plays out as the poem stages cuts both physical and hermeneutic, creating a narrative structure rooted in a spirit/letter duality.

CUTTING THE TEXTUAL BODY

Subtly, the poem depicts the Green Knight's decapitation as a hermeneutic event. When the Green Knight bends down in order to receive Gawain's blow, "a littel lut with þe hede, þe lere he discouerez," and he "let þe naked nec to þe note schewe" ("with his head bent a little, uncovers the flesh"; "let the bare neck show in readiness"; ll. 418, 420). Gawain brings the axe "doun liyȝtly lyȝt on þe naked" ("down quickly on the bare flesh"; l. 423). These lines illustrate a process of exposure and discovery—a process like reading. Nakedness implies a hermeneutic unveiling, an exposure.[30] The scene has a certain homoerotic valence. And, by staging a scene of slightly sexualized, male/male violence, the poem gestures toward a theory of reading as circumcision—of reading in terms of a violence visited by men upon the male genitals.[31] Unsatisfied by the Knight's nakedness, Gawain executes the extreme letter of their forward. By beheading the Knight, Gawain over-zealously enacts the covenant and stages a scene of excessive literalism, of what I might call circumcision in the letter.

The Knight's decapitation and Gawain's nick both take place upon the flesh, but the former seems much more carnal than the latter and also much less redemptive. Gawain's act of legalistic circumcision corresponds with a moral failure, as the poem later depicts it. Gawain errs primarily because he assumes that his virtue exists as an external performance and that sin exists somewhere external to himself.[32] Gawain sees his virtue as an external item, an external reputation, like an adornment.[33] Gawain mistakes virtue as an outward act, as a law in the flesh. For now, Gawain overzealously executes the letter of his covenant; later, Gawain's transformation will occur when he internalizes the Pauline lesson that circumcision is of the heart.

Curiously, after the Knight has issued his fantastic response to Gawain, the poem then considers the hermeneutic problem of outer display and inner meaning. The poem projects this problem upon another male body, the body of Arthur. But Arthur develops an inner posture at odds with his outer appearance. Other members of the court openly express their fear of the Knight (ll. 442–43). And they make "bare" their wonder (l. 465). But Arthur hides his true feelings: "Thagh Arther the hende kyng at hert hade wonder, / He let no semblaunt be sene" ("If Arthur the noble king was amazed at heart, he let no sign be seen"; ll. 467–68). Manly stoicism appears in *SGGK* as a consequence of the Knight's decapitation. Gawain's literalist circumcision reproduces the schism between outer performance and interior attitude. In this way, the poem explores how a fleshly mode of hermeneutic circumcision can become an embodied practice of hypocrisy. Its meditations on the divergence between inner and outer echo the distinction between inner and outer circumcision, themes explored in *Cleanness* through retellings of Old Testament stories (as I will discuss later in this chapter).

The poem also associates Arthur's rhetorical stance with the performing arts: Arthur rationalizes the Knight's appearance by comparing the Knight to the traditional entertainments of Christmas (ll. 471–75). And the strophe also concerns itself with sign theory: The court places the Knight's axe about the dais, so that it may provide the "trwe tytel" of the marvel ("true right"; l. 480). The hermeneutic exercise of the Knight's circumcision has recapitulated the theme of male contradiction (introduced in the first strophe), and now the poem projects that problem onto an assortment of art forms—theatrical crafts, courtly humans, and symbolic weapons—as though to suggest that Gawain's overly carnal execution of the covenant has precipitated a semiotic problem. In light of the law, meaning becomes a vexed question, whose probing Gawain's journey will narrativize. And, in the final reckoning, Gawain will find some insight into his inner meaning.

The opening scene vernacularizes Paul's notion that the inner and outer may stand starkly at odds, and it sets in motion Gawain's quest. Like Peter's vision or the case of the boy with the long foreskin, *SGGK* is ultimately concerned with a hermeneutic question. Asking about the essential meaning beneath the surface, the poem offers something of a revelation at its climax. Gawain's cut—like the decapitation of the Green Knight—stages a hermeneutic circumcision, but one of a more spiritual character. In order to appreciate the hermeneutic implications of the nick on Gawain's neck, I first track the narrative process that leads to the climax at the Green Chapel, and then I read the nick.

FLESHING OUT THE TEXT

In the previous section, I laid out my case for reading *SGGK*—and particularly its form and structure—in terms of a literary theory of circumcision. I suggested that the poet initially constructs the poem's textual body as masculine and double and that the Knight's decapitation stages a literal circumcision. I also suggested that the nick on Gawain's neck stages a spiritual circumcision, so that the narrative charts Gawain's progression from a literalist to a spiritual reader. And I suggested that the poem links its doubled structures with the occasion of the Circumcision, creating hermeneutic layers akin to the literal/spiritual dualism of the exegetical method described by Paul through metaphors of circumcision.

Now, in this section, I will consider the narrative elements that occur between these two cuts, and then I will more fully explore Gawain's nick. I will zoom in on instances where the poet employs preputial forms (specifically wit, amplification, and chiastic structures), and I will explain how these preputial forms track a circumlogical scheme—a narratological program—based on Pauline hermeneutics. I will trace how the poet narrates the body of the poem through a process whereby the text becomes increasingly fleshly, in order that the poem's climax can create a kind of spiritual circumcising of this textual body.

In fitt 1, the poem's first circumcision marks Gawain's entry into a covenant that I described as vexed by semiotic anxiety. The execution of a legalistic circumcision propels Gawain toward his *wyrd* and into the ethical trap of the green girdle's prisoner's dilemma. In fitt 2, as Gawain ventures toward his destiny, he becomes the amplified subject of several strophes that richly describe his gear.[34] These amplifications narrate a development of Gawain's exteriority as a hypocritical, fleshy legalism, as a courtly masculinity performed in the outer letter.

A wheel insinuates a correspondence between the "ways" of storytelling and the "ways" of the knight's journey:

> He made non abode
> Bot wy3tly went hys way.
> Mony wylsum way he rode
> Þe bok as I herde say.

(He made no delay but swiftly went on his way. He rode many uncertain paths, as I learned from the book; ll. 687–90)

Rhyme and repetition render the knight's adventure as roughly analogous to the words of the book. Turning away from the exposition in Camelot, the plot begins to rise, and the story, like Gawain, begins to wind on a wylsum way.

This path leads to Bertilak's castle—a space often correlated with the human body in medieval allegory.[35] Some readers have suggested that Bertilak's castle is phallic.[36] But with "chalk-whyt chymnées" ("chalk-white chimneys") and embrasures "pared out of papure" ("cut out of paper"; ll. 798, 802), the body of the castle becomes a piece of ephemera, a cartoon drawing. Masculinity disintegrates, and, inside the castle, female bodies begin to feminize the text.

Now the narrative reenters the world of the court. As the bodies of Morgan and Lady Bertilak receive considerable attention, the body of the poem undergoes a transformation. Previously, the poem had rendered the best knights of Camelot with linear, superlative descriptions. Now, *SGGK* renders these two female bodies with chiastic, comparative descriptions. The bodies of the old Morgan and the young Lady Bertilak may represent typologically the Old and the New Laws.[37] But Sir Gawain does not perceive these bodies according to the Pauline theory of hermeneutic circumcision, which would render them allegorically equivalent. Instead, Gawain regards the figures as dualistic opposites.

Camelot's court had held "þe lovelokkest ladies" ("the loveliest ladies") as well as "þe most kyd knyghtes" ("the most renowned knights") and "þe comlokest kyng" ("the finest king"; ll. 52–54). But in Bertilak's castle, the female figures invite comparison: "unlyke on to loke þo ladyes were" ("those ladies were dissimilar in appearance"; l. 950). To Gawain, Lady Bertilak appears "wener þen Wenore" ("lovelier than Guinevere"), a pun that establishes female identity as somehow fundamentally comparative (l. 945). With another comparative, Gawain sees Morgan as "alder" ("older") than Lady Bertilak (l. 948).

Contrasting these two bodies, the stanza assumes a chiastic structure.[38] One line constitutes an antithesis, and two subsequent lines together create another antithesis:

For if þe ȝonge watz ȝep, ȝolȝe watz þat oþer;
Riche red on þat on rayled ayquere,
Rugh ronkled chekez þat oþer on rolled.

(For if the young one was blooming, the other was sallow; a glowing pink everywhere adorned the first one, rough wrinkled cheeks sagged on the other; ll. 951–53)

Antitheses formally embody a kind of feminine entanglement.[39] In these lines, repetition of the word "on" poetically conflates the two women, while the rhetorical structure tries to distinguish them. The rest of the strophe fleshes out these two bodies in an extended, unbalanced antithesis, in which the loathly Morgan overwhelms the device. But the wheel's quick rhythm switches attention back to the body of Lady Bertilak, who, by comparison, looks "more lykkerwys on to lyk" ("more delicious to taste"; l. 968). The wheel's shape, which formerly had harmonized opposites in ambiguous interrelatedness, now cuts opposites apart through comparison. From female figures old and young, *SGGK* forms a poetic body of dualistic opposites. And as female bodies dominate the poem, Gawain physically seems to shrink—descriptions of male bodies no longer dominate the text.

If poetic content indicates something about the physical experience of the body of the poem, then the second fitt indicates a change in the poem's body. Fitt 2 marks a transformation: The poem becomes increasingly chiastic in structure, and it becomes increasingly preoccupied with feminine bodies. This second fitt motivates the third fitt, which dilates expansively: The third fitt constitutes over one-third of the total poem (871 lines out of 2,527)—a significant disproportion that in itself shows how this section of the poem becomes narratologically thicker.

Thicker, because the third fitt operates through the chiastic juxtaposition of simultaneous events. In fitt 2, the poem used a chiastic structure to describe female bodies. Now, in fitt 3, the poem further realizes chiasmus as a mode of narration. The poet narrates the hunting scenes and the seduction scenes in an interwoven order, with simultaneous events enveloped into one another. The fitt's main narrative technique consists in an alternation between seduction and hunting/butchering, an alternation that chops up the poetic body.[40]

The narrative structure mimics the cutting of the body. As I have argued, the poem's textual body gives shape to its preoccupation with cutting—a preoccupation linked to the Circumcision—and the poem deploys various figures in order to conceptualize the circumcisable body of the text. Having initially constructed the textual body in terms of the male, monstrous body of the Knight, the poem now proceeds to reproduce in poetic form the chopped-up bodies of the beasts—through juxtaposing these bodies against the bodies of Gawain and Lady Bertilak and continually offering the exchange of literal for symbolic, of love tokens for the cut flesh of beasts, a circumcision of the letter for a circumcision of the spirit, with the final token—the green girdle—operating, as in the logic of Christ's Circumcision, as inassimilable to such an exchange and, in the final act, effecting a merciful redemption.

This chiasmic narrative offers a glimpse into the "now" of distended Augustinian temporality (which I discussed in Chapter 2). By giving order to simultaneous nows, the poem's body undertakes a process of temporal distention. This distention is not necessarily the same as the logic by which the "now" of Christian spiritual circumcision supersedes the "then" of Jewish literal circumcision.[41] Yet the syntax of the poem's temporal juxtapositions embodies a temporal relation that implies allegorical equivalence. By thickening the narrative body through temporal juxtaposition, this portion of the poem prepares the textual body to undergo the hermeneutic circumcision that, at the Green Chapel, will reveal the poem's typological structure.

The shape of the poem begins to gesture toward Gawain's final entry into the distended time of allegory.[42]

Fitt 3, I think, implies the allegorical equivalence of its concurrent events: The Exchange of Winnings translates bodies into signs or signs into bodies. The scenes of seduction closely correspond with the hunting scenes. In particular, the fox's reputation for treachery makes him an analogue for Gawain, and, in parallel, both figures meet their judgment precisely because of their tricky attempts to escape.[43] More correspondences occur later in the poem, when the events at the Green Chapel allude to the hunting of the boar.[44] These parallels have to do with the poem's interest in masculinity: The fox turns aside "stiffly," so that the fox's death points to the frailty of "stiff" male bodies, and, relatedly, the "lovely unlacing" of the boar echoes both the "love-lace" and the cut ("lace") that Gawain receives.[45] The poem means to show the vulnerability inherent in masculine stiffness—and in the poem's own textual body, which toggles between the literal flesh of animals and their symbolic equivalents.

During the course of the narrative, the reader only hazily can grasp the connections between the hunting scenes and the seduction scenes.[46] But later, following the final revelations at the Green Chapel, the full significance of the hunting comes into view: They roughly foretell Gawain's fall. As I said, the implicit connections between the hunting scenes and the seduction scenes create a temporal thickening that motivates the typological revelation at the Green Chapel. The two series are linked by the forward and by the parallelisms implicit in their situations.[47] The forward—in its covenantal connotations—provides the framework for the symbolic parallels that grant access to typological temporality. The technique of interlacing embodies a kind of narratological preputiality, a distention of narratological temporality into typology. The Exchange of Winnings creates a kind of witticism, an allegorical structure.[48]

Note also that the third fitt enmeshes Gawain in feminine textuality. The poem depicts Lady Bertilak's body and thereby produces the feminine body of language.[49] In the passages that depict the conversations between Lady Bertilak and Sir Gawain, the poem uses syntax and verbal similarities to intertwine the two characters.[50] This formally eroticizes the text.[51] Relatedly, in the temptation scenes, the lines vary markedly from the poem's metrical norms.[52] As the textual body transforms, Gawain receives instruction from

Lady Bertilak about the gender of language. Now, Lady Bertilak makes her appeal to the "lel" ("loyal") letters of romance. As noted previously, Lady Bertilak discourses on "þe lel layk of luf, þe lettrure of armes," and she claims that "hit is þe tytelet token and tyxt of her werkkez / How ledez for her lele luf hor lyuez han auntered" (ll. 1513, 1515–16). Lady Bertilak attempts to account for the heterogeneous gender of human experience and, relatedly, of textuality. Seeing romance as a model for behavior, Lady Bertilak imposes homogeneity upon the textual body. She subordinates all of the elements of a written work—letter and title and text—to one single meaning, embodied by alliteration and apparently obvious at the literal level. Without recourse to allegorical interpretation, text and title and letter all refer monolithically to the union of male and female in fin'amor. Gawain can only confess his poor reading skills (ll. 1540–45).

Fitt 3 narrates the interweaving of two hermeneutic paradigms. My paradigm of the circumlogical text might coexist alongside—and become conflated with—the paradigm of the feminine text.[53] Indeed, as I will explore in my next chapter, medieval theologies described matrimony as a state of uncircumcision, with men's wives coded as foreskins, and the persistent construction of the foreskin as feminine, interarticulated with this curious notion of marriage as uncircumcision, may license a shuttling between these paradigms. If the content of this fitt reveals anything about the textual body, it reveals how the textual body can be apprehended in terms of both heterosexual erotic tension, on the one hand, and in terms of male-male erotic aggression, on the other (the scenes between Gawain and Lady Bertilak interwoven with scenes of hunting).

The poem proposes that, in a certain way, male/female romance can be exchanged with the slaying of beasts by male-dominated groups. And both frameworks can serve relatedly for conceptualizing the body of the text.[54] Both the hunts and the seductions involve a process of assaying—hermeneutic acts related to the ultimate assaying of Gawain.[55] The hunt scenes unravel the poem's heroic thread, while the seduction scenes unravel the romantic thread, with each reconnected by discerning the cut upon Gawain's flesh.[56] In other words, both interwoven plots explore hermeneutic questions: The bodies of the beasts emblematize a certain process of "cutting" in order to discern meaning, while the bodies of Gawain and Lady Bertilak gesture toward a framework in which meaning becomes comprehensible

through male/female romance. As these plots finally intertwine—in a conclusion that Gawain finds regrettable—they ultimately prove unsatisfac-
tory as modes of interpretation. On one level, the exchange of romance for
hunting—of male/female relations for male/male relations—participates in
the Pauline universalism that transcends earthly binaries (like circumcision and uncircumcision) and seeks to resolve difference through spiritual
circumcision.

The Green Chapel elaborates for Gawain a new interpretative technique.
In the fourth fitt, the poem recapitulates its male-foundation fantasies by
using words that recall the first fitt: Gawain's guide to the Green Chapel
describes the Green Knight as "on bent much baret bende" ("caused much
strife on the battlefield") and "borelych burne on bent" ("huge warrior who
keeps [the valley]"), and Gawain laments his "trecherye and vntrawþe"
("treachery and dishonesty"; ll. 2115, 2148, 2383). These lines hark back to the
truly treacherous founding of Britain: "Ande quen þis Bretayn watz bigged
bi þis burn ryche, / Bolde bredden þerinne, baret þat lofden" (ll. 20–21).

Then, the nick on the neck more fully exposes how the poem's surface
has hidden a secret kernel of meaning. Bertilak reveals to Gawain that he
had engineered Lady Bertilak's trick and that Morgan had engineered the
entire spectacle. The nick upon Gawain's neck exposes the hidden, typological structure that gives meaning to the poem's main characters. It reveals to Gawain the distinction between his true essence and his reputation
(Bertilak calls the process an "assay"; l. 2362). And it reveals the distinction
between Lady Bertilak's appearance and her true intent, as well as the duality of Bertilak/Green Knight and Morgan/Loathly Lady. The nick produces
a circumcision upon the body of the poem, so that its hidden, typological
workings become apparent—a circumlogical allegoresis.

The four poems in the manuscript are not all allegorical narratives, but
all rely on allegorical thinking.[57] Clearly, SGGK does not deal in allegorical
personifications.[58] Rather than constructing a psychomachia, the Gawain-
Poet develops a basically literal story, whose protagonist, in the moment of
climax, turns to allegoresis as a mode of self-understanding—a turn that
simultaneously rereads the whole text in an allegorical sense.

Moreover, at this climax, Gawain speaks at a metanarrative level, reciting
his transgressions. Crucially, at exactly this moment, the poem undertakes
its only critical engagement with the Bible. SGGK rarely refers to the Bible.[59]

But once nicked, Gawain undertakes a kind of autoexegesis. Gawain reads himself in light of biblical types, claiming that he, like other great men, has fallen victim to treacherous women:

> For so watz Adam in erde with one bygyled,
> And Salamon with fele sere, and Samson, eftsonez—
> Dalyda dalt hym hys wyrde—and Dauyth þerafter,
> Watz blended with Barsabe, þat much bale þoled.
> Now þese were wrathed wyth her wyles, hit were a wynne huge
> To luf hom wel and leue hem not, a leude þat couthe.

(For so was Adam of old beguiled by one, and Solomon by many different [ones], and Samson, again—Delilah mete out his fate to him—and similarly David was deluded by Bathsheba, and endured much sorrow. Since these were troubled by their wiles, it would be a great advantage to love them well and not trust them, if a man could; ll. 2416–21)

Gawain cites five male biblical figures and their female counterparts, all from the Old Testament. Perhaps Gawain's speech represents an ignorant reliance upon an established, antifeminist rhetoric.[60] Or perhaps Gawain simply invokes the fact of his personal experience.[61] In either case, the nick has taught Gawain to become an allegorical reader, one who views personal experience as typologically linked with biblical antecedent.

Now, Gawain sees himself as the recipient of spiritual tradition, derived from biblical forefathers—rather than seeing himself (as the poem previously insinuated) as the descendent of Trojans. The circumcision of the nick makes him, at least spiritually, a kind of Jew "in the heart" (a Christian whose spiritual life draws inspiration from interpreted Jewish texts).

Gawain's nick coincides with his sudden understanding of how flesh fails to signify the spiritual. Now he looks inward: "so agreved for greme he gryed withinne" ("so overcome with vexation that he shuddered within"; l. 2370). And he laments "the faute and the fayntyse of the flesche crabbed" ("the sinfulness and fallibility of the perverse flesh"; l. 2435). The girdle, he claims, will serve as a reminder that he must privilege the heart about the flesh: "the loke to this luf-lace schal lethe my heart" ("looking at this love-girdle will humble my heart"; l. 2438). As the body of the poem undergoes hermeneutic circumcision, the protagonist himself becomes aware of inner meaning.

Gawain locates his personal experience within a circumcised typological imaginary.[62] And Gawain begins to read beneath the surface, proposing a paradoxical hermeneutics: to "luf hom wel and leue hem not"—an idea Pauline in its paradoxical form, if not in its sentiment (l. 2421). Like Troilus, who in death realizes that meaning transcends the body—that the "uncircumscript" Trinity "al mayst circumscryve"—so, too, the circumcised Gawain realizes himself, like even the best of men, as open to interpretation, like a biblical text circumfused by marginal commentary.[63] With the cut, the poem and its protagonist articulate the view, articulated by Boccaccio, that fables contain "meaning or intention hidden beneath the superficial veil of myth."[64] Gawain's girdle resembles the Pauline *praeputium*: As an equivocal sign—a source of both shame and of comedy—the green girdle ambiguously signifies one thing publicly and another internally.

I haven't said enough about temporality. With the nick, the threads of the poem converge, with the anticipated forward finally realized. The two, interlinked New Year's Feasts (though chronologically separated) now fold into each other, as though through a fulfilled prophecy. The poem is trying to put into narrative form what happens when time is spiritually circumcised.

In my analysis of *SGGK*, I have employed circumcision as a heuristic for conceptualizing the poem's narrative structure. The poem frames its typological concerns in terms of the Circumcision, so that its narrative trajectory models the process of Pauline conversion from literal to spiritual circumcision. This reading has several implications, two of which I will detail next. First, I will explore how the circumlogical structure of *SGGK* allies the poem with the manuscript's other, more clearly homiletic poems, especially *Cleanness*. Second, I will explore how the circumlogical structure of *SGGK* demonstrates an attempt to spiritualize the body of alliterative romance, as part of a process that I will define as *translatio praeputii*.

IMPLICATIONS: CIRCUMCISION IN *CLEANNESS*

Monastics, I have said, used the hermeneutics of circumcision to align monastic habit and interior will, to discipline the monastic body and the body of speech, to "circumcise" the outer and inner lips. This religious, hermeneutic framework structures *SGGK* and runs throughout another poem in the manuscript, *Cleanness*.

In *Cleanness*, Noah receives the sign of the rainbow, "Myryly on a fayr morn, monyth the first,/That falles formast in the yer, and the first day" ("on a fine morning on the first day in the first month that falls first in the year"; ll. 493–94). The first day of the first month of the year is, of course, the first of January—the same day upon which Gawain decapitates the Knight and upon which, one year later, Gawain receives his nick. In the context of *SGGK*, the occasion of the Circumcision frames the poem's typological concerns. The events of *Cleanness*—strictly speaking—take place long before the birth of Christ, and so the Feast of the Circumcision has not yet been established (indeed, the events of *Cleanness* take place even before the establishment of the circumcision). And God's covenant with Noah anticipates God's covenant with Abraham, as well as the new covenant of Christianity.[65] In *Cleanness*, God creates what he calls a "forwarde" with Noah (l. 327).[66] By keying Noah's covenant to January 1 and by describing it as a forward, the *Gawain*-Poet links this covenant with the events of *SGGK*.[67]

Both *Cleanness* and *SGGK* engage the circumlogical question of inner posture and outer appearance. *Cleanness* constructs Noah's covenant as spiritual rather than fleshly, through his symbolic comparison of the raven and the dove: The "untrew" raven clearly represents carnality as it "falles on the foule flesch and fylles his wombe" ("falls on the foul flesh and fills his belly"; ll. 456, 462). The dove—symbol of the Spirit—brings to Noah the olive branch, a "sygne of savyté." Echoing the "sygne" given to Gawain, this sign, like the girdle, represents an act of mercy and a moment of ambivalence. God accepts that men are wicked in their wits and in their hearts (ll. 514–15). But God nevertheless promises not to destroy humanity—using the same language employed to describe the cuts of *SGGK*: "Forthy schal I never *schende* so schortly at ones" ("Therefore I shall never punish . . . so hastily . . . everything at once"; *Cleanness*, l. 519, emphasis mine).

Noah receives his covenantal sign on the "fayr morn" of New Year's Day. These words recall the poem's opening stanza, which describes how a person seeking to discuss cleanness must find "fayre formes" (l. 3). In its exploration of cleanness, the poem repeatedly employs the word "fayre" in order to point to how outer fairness may or may not correspond with actual, inner purity. The devil's hypocrisy, for example, takes the form of "fayre wedes" (l. 217). And men "fairest of forme" and women "derelych fayre" actually incite sin with their beauty (ll. 253, 269). Noah, on the other hand, sets up a "fayre" altar (l. 506). Early in its exploration of this theme, the poem observes the Pauline truth that outer observance of the law might betray inner hypocrisy:

> Bot if they conterfete crafte and cortaysye wont,
> As be honest utwyth and inwith alle fylthes,
> Then ar thay sinful himself, and sulped altogeder
> Bothe God and his gere, and hym to greme cachen.

(But if they feign wisdom and lack courtesy, by being pure on the outside and all filth within, then they are sinful themselves and altogether defile both God and His utensils, and drive to him wrath; ll. 13–16)

The need for both outer and inner purity is, from the outset, the main prerogative of the poem. Throughout, *Cleanness* insists that true purity exists in the "heart" (e.g., ll. 516, 575, 593–94). The tension between outer and inner purity generates much of the narrative momentum.

This tension also motivates the poem's inclination to allegorize. As *Cleanness* illustrates with the parable of the courtiers, it spotlights how outer and inner purity may interrelate, as in the line "bothe withinne and withouten, in wedes ful bryght" ("in very bright clothes . . . both within and without"; l. 20). And, again, the poet insists that outer purity must coincide with inner purity: "for he that flemus uch fylthe fer fro his hert / may not byde that burre, that hit his body neghe" ("for He that banishes all filth from His heart cannot endure the shock of its approaching Him"; ll. 31–32). Within this parable, outer clothing becomes an allegory for spiritual purity, and the poet makes sure that the clothes are understood in their spiritual valence, saying of the poorly clad man "and if unwelcum he were to a worthlych prynce, / Yet hym is the hyghe kyng harder in heven" ("And if he would be unwelcome to an earthly prince, the high King in heaven is even harder to him"; ll. 49–50). Furthermore, the poem undertakes a sermonizing allegoresis that explains the parable:

> Wich arn thenne thy wedes thou wrappes the inne,
> That schal schewe hem so schene, schrowde of the best?
> Hit arn thy werkes wyterly that thou wroght haves,
> And lined with the lykyng that lye in thyn hert.

(What then are your clothes in which you wrap yourself, which must appear like lovely garments of the best? They are your deeds, surely, that

you have done, and lined with the inclination that lay in your heart;
ll. 169–72)

The alliance of outer purity and inner purity produces what the poet again
calls a "fayr forme" (l. 174).

Also, the poem says of Matthew's Gospel that it "of clannesse uncloses
a ful cler speche" ("discloses a clear statement about cleanness"; l. 26). And
Matthew teaches how "the hathel of clene of his hert hapenes ful fayre" ("It
turns out very well for the man with a clean heart"; l. 27). By unclosing this
message of spiritual cleanness within the fair form of clear speech, Matthew practices the kind of linguistic circumcision proposed by Augustine,
in which outer and inner lips both are purified.

Ultimately, *Cleanness*'s critique of hypocrisy may derive from debates
about legalism.[68] This legalism explains in part the failure of Gawain, as well
as the *Pearl*-dreamer's misunderstanding of merit and the overall agenda of
Cleanness.[69] My reading of *SGGK* connects its moral allegory with the circumlogical concerns of *Cleanness*, as that poem also thinks about the inner
and the outer levels of meaning by way of covenantal theology.

CIRCUMCISING ROMANCE

In *Cleanness*, the *Gawain*-Poet celebrates fair forms—forms that align both
the outer and the inner layers of textuality with ideals of spiritual purity.
This may provide further insight into the structure of *SGGK* and of romance.[70] My reading has suggested that *SGGK* interarticulates femininity
with uncircumcision—and that the poem's critique of excess is a critique
not of femininity but of literalism, expressed through feminine figures and
through vehicles like the beasts and the armor worn by Gawain.

In shearing off this preputiality through entry into allegory, the poem
does not take a position against physical excess per se but against an interior
uncircumcision.[71] Formally, *SGGK* actually cherishes physicality. Highly in-
tricate, *SGGK* evinces a Gothic zest for ornamentation. The poet of *SGGK*
crafts physical phenomena into long, exquisitely adorned lists that divide
bodies into their component parts. Ekphrastic set pieces relish in the pleasures of sumptuous banquets, fine clothes, and extravagantly decorated fa-
cades and interiors. The poem adorns, orders, and beautifies its body. What
it seeks is not, then, moralistically to sheer off of fleshly excess but to ac-

complish a spiritual circumcision that allies the outer body of romance with interior Christian ideals.

Alliteration beefs up the poetic body. More than almost any other literary technique, alliteration's cacophony of consonants calls upon the corporeality of language. And the Middle English alliterative line differs from the Old English alliterative line in ways that enhance this corporeality. Middle English lines often alliterate on the fourth stress (a feature forbidden by the Old English scops), and Middle English lines license extra alliteration and an occasional fifth prominence position—features that make the line fatter.[72] These developments create a different kind of alliterative architecture. Old English poems braid appositional phrases into interlacing rings, creating textual meshes that resemble Anglo-Saxon artifacts.[73] In Middle English alliteration poetry, the syntactically complete, end-stopped lines bulge with ornamentation, creating a flexible linearity typical of Gothic architecture. With this style, Middle English alliterative poems craft thick and meaty descriptions of the physical world.

Alliterative poems engage in conspicuous consumption. In *Cleanness*, for example, the poet offers a lesson about spiritual purity through a lengthy parable about wearing appropriate attire to a lavish feast (ll. 29–164). Even when fourteenth-century alliterative poets critique bodily pleasures, they do so in a style that thrills at bodily excess—much like the friar in *Piers Plowman*, who lectures about fasting while he overeats (C.15.86–95). Describing the sin of gluttony, William Langland poetically overindulges, referring to urination in relation to the "Our Father." Of Gluttony, Langland writes,

A Pissed a potel in a Paternoster-whyle
And blew his rownde ruet at his rygebones ende,
That alle þat herde þe horne helde here nose aftur,
And wesched hit hadde be wexed with a weps of breres . . .
Ac Gloton was a greet cherl and greued in þe luftynge,
And cowed up a caudel in Clementis lappe.
Ys none so hungry hound in Hertfordshyre
Durste lape of þat lyuynge, so vnlouely hit smauhte!
(He pissed half a gallon in the time of a *pater noster*,
He blew his round bugle at his backbone's bottom,
So that all who heard that horn had to hold their noses
And wished it had been well plugged with a wisp of briars.

But Glutton was a huge boor and troubled in the lifting
And barfed up a mess into Clement's lap;
There is no hound so hungry in Hertfordshire
That he'd dare lap up that leaving, so unlovely it smacked!)[74]

Alliteration binges on words. Like Glutton's butt trumpet, alliteration turns gross smells into raunchy sounds, coughing up consonants like pools of plosive puke.

Alliterative excess also lends itself to narrative excess—most obviously in the case of Langland.[75] SGGK, in contrast with Piers, manages its proportions. But, in the case of SGGK, hermeneutic circumcision disciplines the poetic body. Initially established as male and subsequently complicated by female figures, the form of the poem undergoes a circumcision that draws its plot toward a tidy conclusion. Just as the stanzaic structure allows for the ordering of physical excesses, the plot's cuts manage the romantic genre. Arthurian works (before Malory) typically ramble from one adventure to the next, with each episode related in a piecemeal fashion, so that the composition as a whole creates relatively little cohesion or overarching suspense.[76]

Digressions, amplifications, and a general lack of unity typify the genre.[77] Unlike many medieval romances, SGGK does not meander episodically, nor does Gawain play the knight-errant. A man on a mission, Gawain pursues a single destiny, a wyrd preordained since the beginning. By compassing its plot to the Feast of the Circumcision, SGGK disciplines the body of romance and achieves dramatic unity. Note that I am neither for nor against dramatic unity; I am just trying to explain how the underlying, theo-poetic principle of circumcision is at work in developing this unity.

The poem's final line recalls its opening line. This shape realizes the poem's pessimistic take on history and manhood.[78] But the encounter at the Green Chapel also provides a lesson in mercy, and the final scene of the poem strikes a comedic note. Having become circumcised in the Pauline sense, Gawain can undertake his shriving iteratively. Pauline circumcision and uncircumcision interrelate dialectically, in ways that strict binaries do not, since the dialectic, as a process, allows for endless repetition. The "endless knot" of the poem's structure creates a cycle that moves from sin to grace (or from sin to sin or grace to grace), so that the body of the poem entangles inexplicably together circumcision and uncircumcision, spirit and letter, form and content.

In trying to bring new attention to formal questions, I have also reevaluated the notion that medieval people saw textuality as feminine. In my reading of *SGGK*, I have introduced a bridge between these two schemes: The poem's circumlogical structure plays out through the interaction of gendered figures, so that the poem works toward rethinking the preputial veil of allegory as feminine. The poem disciplines the body of romance.[79] By connecting its climactic allegoresis to the Feast of the Circumcision, *SGGK* translates the patristic, hermeneutic foreskin into a vernacular register, and, as it does so, the poem projects the *praeputium* into a different gender matrix.

Whereas patristic theory is maybe preoccupied with the male/male erotic violence of circumcision, vernacular romance is preoccupied with male/ female erotic seduction. In the translation from one matrix to another, the textual prepuce becomes enveloped within a heterosexual scheme. But, by using the figure of Sir Gawain to finally circumcise the poem's textual body, the poem becomes aligned with circumcised, chaste ideals. The poem produces, ultimately, a masculine hero whose salvation follows from his failures and whose exemplarity results from the vulnerability of his body.

I said that, in a certain way, Gawain's nick reconfigures his patrilineal ancestry. In citing Old Testament precedents for his own failure, Gawain identifies himself in relation to Jewish ancestors (whereas the poem previously had traced Camelot's lineage from Troy to Rome to Brutus). If, in that opening passage, the poem joins the patrilineal poetic history of the alliterative tradition, then the poem—in its climactic nick—also reconfigures its own ancestry. Alliterative romances like *SGGK* may have revived old forms in order to explore new problems.[80] On the occasion of the Feast of the Circumcision, which typologically interrelates old and new, the poem performs a hermeneutic circumcision that reads the alliterative tradition into a Jewish/Christian ancestry. I will explore this more in my next chapter, which reads "The Wife of Bath's Tale" through theologies that theorized the circumcision of marriage.

CHAPTER FOUR

THE FORESKIN OF MARRIAGE

> Well, is wantonness to be encouraged in youth, so that in later life it may be the more fully rejected? "Heaven forbid!" they say, for "let every man, wherein he is called, therein abide." "Is any called being circumcised—that is, a virgin—let him not become uncircumcised"—that is, let him not seek in marriage the coats of skins wherewith Adam clothed himself when he was expelled from the paradise of virginity. "Is any called in uncircumcision—that is, having a wife and covered with the skin of matrimony: let him not seek the nakedness of virginity and of that eternal chastity which he has forfeited once for all."
>
> —Saint Jerome, Letter to Pacatula

One of the stars of the show in Chaucer's *The Canterbury Tales*, the Wife of Bath has become a special favorite among modern readers—after all, who doesn't love a sex-positive, entrepreneurial gal?[1] My own students are always pleasantly surprised that a fourteenth-century poet like Chaucer could develop, in the Prologue to the Wife's Tale, such a vivacious and apparently feministic portrait of a woman who, loving to screw, has married five times and, in the process, amassed a small fortune and launched a powerful business. But in short order, those same students become turned off, appalled even, when they read the Wife's Tale, which—seeming to reverse course—is about the redemption of a male rapist (a knight who, on pain of death for his crime, must seek the truth of "what women want," and only finds the answer after a hideous fairy agrees to tell him the secret, but only if he agrees to marry her). The story gets weirder still when the fairy, having saved the knight's life and having become his wife, offers to transform into a beautiful woman, who, she says, may well cheat on him; or, she could, she says, remain ugly but be faithful. When the knight allows the fairy to decide for herself—thus proving that he has internalized the need for female autonomy—the fairy gives him *both* beauty and fidelity—a move that my students frankly see as

82

double-dealing, since the knight really had no options, anyway. And if all of this were not funky enough, let me throw a foreskin into the mix!

The Canterbury Tales makes no overt references to circumcision. Yet the Wife's Tale shares many structural similarities with *SGGK*.[2] The Wife's Tale, like *SGGK*, begins with an overly aggressive knight who commits a wicked deed, and this knight then must enter into a year-long agreement. After the poem tracks the wayward wanderings of this carnal protagonist, he ends up being saved by a turn to allegorical interpretation. Moreover, at least one early reader of the Wife had understood her as a *praeputium*: An early manuscript glosses her with a patristic commentary on how wives are like foreskins.[3]

As I suggested, patristic thinkers often conceptualized literalism and carnality through metaphors of uncircumcision, and theologians oppose these preputial figures to the spiritual circumcision of allegorical interpretation. Also, I said that Jerome imagined a man's marriage to a woman as a state of uncircumcision—a simile that implies a correspondence between women and foreskins. And, relatedly, Paul denied not only the distinction between Jew and Greek but also the distinction between male and female, so that Paul's circumcising hermeneutics would spiritualize the genital differences between circumcised and uncircumcised, as well as the genital differences between male and female (Gal. 3:28). Conceptual metaphors of the foreskin do not preclude the possibility that medieval people also regarded the physical/literal as feminine and the spiritual/allegorical as masculine. Rather, figures of uncircumcision might meaningfully intersect with late medieval gender dynamics. As in *SGGK*, where circumcision's transcendental power opens up the possibility for a universalism that exchanges male/female and male/male, the circumcision of marriage may provide a vocabulary for describing how the *Tales* interrelate men, women, and hermeneutics.[4]

Tropes of circumcision enabled the medieval ennobling of marriage. As I showed previously, the Circumcision of Christ—as a major, typologically determined moment in his *vita*—played a role in some descriptions of the mystagogy of marriage. Furthermore, by spiritually circumcising this fleshly institution, I said, medieval thinkers found a way to sacramentalize an institution that queerly refused to find a neat place in a scheme that categorized the sacraments in terms of the Old and the New. By ordering marriage toward the Augustinian good, spouses (like those in the *Chevrot*

Altarpiece) could excise the "foreskin" that, according to Jerome, might cover a marriage—the fleshly elements of matrimony, not only coitus but also the worldly goods possibly obtained through marriage.

MARRIAGE AND CIRCUMCISION

In sundry lands and in sundry ages, humans have often associated circumcision with marriage—by performing circumcision as a preparation for marriage, by using one word to refer to both rites (as in Hebrew and Arabic), and by deploying circumcision as a kind of wedding ritual with the divinity.[5] Medieval Christians, as I will show here, sometimes thought about marriage as a "foreskin" that needed to be spiritually circumcised. In Paul's first letter to the Corinthians, the Apostle denied the significance of ethnicity, gender, and slavery. Curiously, Saint Jerome imploded all three of these figures and read them as equivalent: "Whoever has a wife," Jerome wrote, "so that he is called a debtor and is said to be uncircumcised, and the slave of his wife."[6]

Later, the understanding of the fleshiness of marriage as a foreskin became complicatedly interrelated to the (similarly circumlogical) divide between Judaism and Christianity. In the twelfth century, Hugh of Saint-Victor played a major role in developing a theology of conjugal marriage. Hugh's theory of marriage relies upon Paul's distinction between the letter and the spirit.[7] Hugh explains that marriage has a twofold cause: "one before sin, as an office; and one after sin, as a remedy."[8] Hugh, drawing upon Augustine, argues that, before the Fall, God instituted marriage as an office for the mingling of flesh and for the generation of offspring. In a postlapsarian world, this same institution becomes a remedy for sexual weakness: "In marriage, marriage itself is something, and the sacrament something else; and the office of marriage is one thing, and the sacrament something else." Hugh distinguishes between the letter and the spirit of marriage.[9]

Hugh explained that the office of marriage must undergo a kind of spiritualization in order to attain sacramentality. For Hugh, marriage counts as a sacrament only when it aligns with spiritual ends.[10] The sacramentalization of conjugal marriage involved just such a circumcision.

Around the same period, Peter Lombard further defined matrimony in a way that enabled its conceptualization through circumcision. The Lombard understood matrimony and circumcision as inverse exceptions to the Old

Law/New Law paradigm. In his treatment of the sacraments, the Lombard distinguished between "signs" and "sacraments" by developing an idea put forth by Hugh.[11] The Lombard followed Hugh in teaching that sacraments, as distinct from signs, actually confer the grace that they signify. For Hugh, this distinction paralleled the division between the Old Law and the New, since the sacraments of the New Law conferred grace, whereas the sacraments of the Old Law acted as allegorical signs of the Gospels.[12] So, "the sacraments of the Old Law," according to the Lombard, "are improperly called sacraments."[13] The circumlogical hermeneutics that structures the Old/New division impinges upon this emerging understanding of the sacraments, except that, within Hugh's paradigm, the Lombard noted two noted exceptions: circumcision and marriage.

For the Lombard, Old Law circumcision conferred a remedy against sin, much like baptism under the New Law.[14] Circumcision thus resembles a New Law sacrament, since circumcision rises above the level of a mere sign (since it *also* acts as a remedy). Contrariwise, marriage differs from the other New Law sacraments, which all confer grace, because marriage in itself does not confer grace (since it *only* acts as a remedy). The good of marriage consists primarily in protecting against sin, as Augustine attests in *De bono coniugali* ("On the Good of Marriage"). In the Lombard's discussion of the sacraments, marriage resembles circumcision because both have a merely remedial efficacy.[15] Circumcision surpasses the standards of the Old Law, while marriage falls below the standards of the New Law—so that both are inverse exceptions to the paradigm.[16] Peter of Poitiers notes that marriage existed before the New Law, and this fact, for Peter, excuses how marriage seems to contradict the principle that sacraments of the New Law will cause what they signify.[17]

EXAMPLES OF CIRCUMCISED MARRIAGE

As medieval theologians theorized companionate marriage, and indeed as lay people put companionate marriage into practice, the emerging notion of marital affection consisted of an inner reality and an outer expression.[18] This dynamic necessitated a circumcision of marriage that would align the interior life with the external rite.

The circumlogical queerness of matrimony—its inverted nature, as a sacrament, in relation with the circumcised/uncircumcised binary of Jewish letter and Christian spirit, along with its flesh/spirit hermeneutic structure, in need of snipping—is especially well illustrated in the *Chevrot Altarpiece* (1450), which depicts matrimony as unique among the sacraments because of its distinct relationship with the Old Testament. The painting shows seven angels holding scrolls above each of the seven sacraments. All of these texts derive from the New Testament, except one—the text for Matrimony.[19]

This text claims that Christ only "commends" certain marriages. Above the marrying couple, the scroll (citing the Old Testament) reads, "Christ commended marriage, provided that the bloody bride be bound in the flesh."[20] The altarpiece suggests that each marriage needs to undergo some manner of transformation—a binding—that makes the marriage commendable.[21] Spiritual circumcision ennobles marriage.

Notably, the phrase "blood bride" derives from Exodus, in which Zipporah circumcises her son and chastises her husband, Moses, as a "bloody bridegroom." Through circumcision, Zipporah won God's commendation for her husband and for her marriage. Intertextually, the scroll prescribes a circumcision of marriage.

"Husbands, love your wives," Paul wrote, "as Christ also loved the church, and delivered himself for it . . . that he might sanctify it, cleansing it" (Eph. 5: 25–26). This passage from Ephesians commonly circulated as evidence that the sacrament of marriage signified the union of Christ and the church. As reread by the hymn, marriage becomes sanctified by the Circumcision and the Crucifixion. As Ambrose said, Christ first bled at his bris, and the Holy Prepuce became a kind of wedding ring exchanged between Christ and the church: Christ wed his bride through Circumcision. God's commendation of marriage depends upon circumcision. Christ's Circumcision underwrites the mystagogy of marriage, with the blood of the Circumcision cleansing it.[22]

Saint Catherine of Siena wrote that "on the eighth day, when he was circumcised, [he] gave up just so much flesh to make a tiny circlet of a ring."[23] Christ offered his severed shroud to Catherine as a matrimonial band. Alphonsus Salmeron, a close companion of Ignatius of Loyola, founder of the Jesuits, similarly claimed that Christ offered his Prepuce as an engagement ring to his bride, the Church of Rome.[24] The Holy Prepuce is a sign of Christian spiritual marriage. Christ married the church through his Circumcision—a prefatory, prophetic instant in Christian history when Christ, newly

Incarnate, fulfilled the Old Law while simultaneously becoming marked on his own body with the typological sign that heralded the Crucifixion. As the moment that cuts apart the Old and New Laws—distinguishing them while hermeneutically interrelating them—the Circumcision provides a loophole that finesses the theological problem of marriage's Old Law carnality, or marriage as a union both in the letter and in the spirit.

The *Chevrot Altarpiece* participates in a program of circumcising marriage: The painting accepts that Christ commends only those marriages that meet certain standards in which fleshly union undergoes spiritualization. As Hugh had explained, Christ's commendation of a marriage depended upon the couple's spiritual orientation. Preaching to the couple in the painting, Hugh would have clarified that their "binding in the flesh" does not necessitate intercourse. In *De sacramentis*, Hugh specifically argues against this reading of Genesis 2:24 ("They shall be two in one flesh"). Instead, according to the *Chevrot Altarpiece*, Christ commends marriage, "provided that the bloody bride be bound in the flesh," or circumcised spiritually.

This is the same kind of spiritual circumcision that Dante recommends for the married in *The Convivio*:

> To a good and true religious order may they also turn who abide in matrimony, for God would have nought of us in religion save in the heart. And therefore St. Paul says to the Romans: "Not he is a Jew who is so outwardly; nor is that circumcision which is manifested in the flesh; but he is a Jew who is so in secret, and circumcision of the heart, in spirit, not in the letter, is circumcision; the praise whereof is not from men but from God" (373).

For Dante, married people become members of a religious order not outwardly but through a circumcision of the heart. In my next section, I will begin to describe how this circumlogical structure of matrimony underlies the narratology of the Wife of Bath's Tale.

THE WIFE OF BATH AS A FORESKIN

I have argued for thinking about narrative structure in terms of Pauline circumcision. And I have established that many premodern thinkers apprehended marriage through metaphors of circumcision. In my reading of the Wife of Bath's Tale, I propose that a circumlogical narratology—like the kind that spiritually circumcises Gawain—operates within this marriage plot, in order to realize a "circumcision of marriage."

I will argue that the Wife of Bath—in her critique of ecclesiastical authority—engages with a literary theory of the *praeputium* and that her Tale employs a circumcised narratology. I will describe the Wife herself in terms of the gender politics of circumcised hermeneutics.[25] By exploring a gloss that figures the Wife as a foreskin and by examining the Wife's conversation with the Pardoner (a figure whom some critics have already identified as "uncircumcised"), I establish the Wife as preputial. Then, reading the Tale, I examine how the Wife employs a circumlogical narratology in order to try to sacramentalize—or, at least, validate—her vision of marriage. Like the circumcised narratology employed in *SGGK*, which was geared toward promoting a fairly orthodox mode of circumcised male spirituality, the Wife uses a similar narrative structure to reinterpret marriage, though not necessarily in an orthodox way.

THE PORTRAIT OF THE WIFE

In her Tale, the Wife employs a circumlogical narratology in order to perform a kind of circumcision upon marriage—though, as I will explain, she does so in order to validate a vision of marriage that does not conform to the Augustinian good. Some early readers of *The Canterbury Tales* evidently read the Wife in terms of a preputial framework. Notably, the manuscript tradition shows that, in general, glosses on the Prologue cite patristic theology in order to prevent readers from sympathizing with the Wife.[26] But individual glossators differ in their sympathy for the Wife and in their level of patristic engagement.[27] At least one glossator annotated the Wife's Prologue with Jerome's interpretation of marriage as uncircumcision.[28] The Wife declares that she would enjoy marking her husband "on his flesh":

> An housbonde I wol have—I wol nat lette—
> Which shal be bothe my dettour and my thral,
> And have his tribulacion withal
> Upon his flessh, whil that I am his wyf.
> (I say again, a husband I must have,

Who shall be both my debtor and my slave,
And he shall have, so long as I'm his wife,
His "trouble in the flesh.") (ll. 154–57; 154)[29]

The Ellesmere Manuscript glosses this passage with a marginal note citing Jerome, who, as I noted, had equated women with foreskins and called married men uncircumcised. The marginalia reads: "Whoever has a wife is called a debtor, a slave of his wife; and he is said to be uncircumcised."[30] Of course, the Wife engages with *Against Jovinian* in a fairly extensive way.[31] And Chaucer translates Jerome almost verbatim, with the Wife referring to her husbands as "dettour" and "thral" (translating *debitor* and *servus*). "Flessh"—at least according to the glossator—refers to the state of uncircumcision that constitutes (for Jerome) a man's marriage.

Read through the gloss, the Wife proposes to uncircumcise her husband by enslaving him to her fleshly demands. The Wife's flagrant sexuality means not only that her vision of marriage does not conform to the Augustinian goods of marriage but that she literally is interested in foreskins. After all, the Wife does not simply advocate multiple marriages; she also advocates for a kind of pleasure seeking within marriage that does not conform to orthodoxy. This makes the Wife's marriages spiritually and literally uncircumcised.

In a comic sendup of Jerome, the Wife relishes the prospect of turning her husbands into the uncircumcised thralls of fleshly enslavement. And, of course, the Wife enjoys commanding her husbands' literal foreskins. In other words, the Wife's reference to "flesh" becomes a double entendre: "Flesh" refers to the *praeputium* of an unorthodox matrimony as well as to the very literal flesh of the prepuce.

Moreover, it is the *praeputium* of Pauline textuality—the literal level—that underwrites the Wife's exegetical practice. Disagreeing with contemporary commentaries in the *Glossa ordinaria*, the Wife practices an unorthodox literalism.[32] Through her erotically charged pun on "flesh," the Wife ironically insists upon enjoying the prepuce as well as the textual *praeputium*. By ironizing the patristic preoccupation with foreskins, the Wife enacts a kind of rhetorical uncircumcision; that is, she performs a kind of preputial wit that is not oriented, through allegoresis, toward the good of marriage. Since this wit does not align with orthodox spiritual ends, the Wife's pun promulgates a kind of uncut rhetoric.

And the Wife's campy reading of Jerome inspires further play from the Pardoner:

Ye been a noble prechour in this cas.
I was aboute to wedde a wyf; allas!
What sholde I bye it on my flessh so deere?
Yet hadde I levere wedde no wyf to-yeere!
(You make a splendid preacher on this theme.
I was about to wed a wife—but then
Why should my body pay a price so dear?
I'll not wed this nor any other year!) (ll. 165–68; 154).

The Pardoner protests rather too much, claiming that he would marry a woman—except that the Wife has taught him about Jerome's insight. But, as the Wife points out, the Pardoner clearly has other reasons for eschewing matrimony.[33] Reading the Pardoner, the Wife effectively mocks not only the Pardoner himself but also Jerome's celibacy, which Jerome symbolized by the circumcised member. Through the Wife's exchange with the Pardoner, the Wife ridicules the Pardoner's queerness, and, indirectly, she lampoons patristic theology's homoerotic preoccupation with the "flesh" of the praeputium.[34]

In the Wife, the Pardoner seems to see a kindred spirit.[35] Although apparent opposites, both represent cupidity and distorted sexuality.[36] And the Wife's exchange with the Pardoner may further license a circumlogical reading because the Pardoner clings to his circumcised bachelorhood heretically (not out of sincere devotion but out of disordered desire). The Pardoner's moral hypocrisy makes him uncircumcised in the Pauline sense: He preaches a kind of carnal circumcision (telling people to abstain from corporeal vices), but he practices a spiritual uncircumcision.[37] In the Pardoner's Tale, the Pardoner uses allegory for fleshly rather than spiritual ends. The characters of this tale seek a literal Death, only to arrive at a moralistic allegory about how the letter kills. The Pardoner wraps this Pauline allegory within a film of sneering sarcasm. As the Pardoner explains to the other pilgrims, he often tells this fable for immoral reasons (he uses the story as a sermon to trick people into buying indulgences from him, and then he wastes this money on booze and gambling). The Pardoner thus has been called a kind of "inward Jew."[38]

Professing a legalistic moralism, the Pardoner conspicuously wears no hood—"but hood for jolity wore he none" (Gen. Prol., ll. 680; "as for a hood, for comfort he wore none," 20). This sartorial sign of Judaizing circumcision registers the Pardoner's inner sklerokardia. Hoodless "jolity" perverts the spirit of glossing, just as much as the Wife's "jolly body" opposes glossing. A gelding or a mare, the Pardoner declines phallic integrity—hence he realizes Paul's sardonic curse upon circumcisers ("I would they were even cut off!"), and he embodies the conflation of circumcision and castration theorized by Freud (Gal. 5:12).[39] Sexually ambiguous and morally reprehensible, sartorially shorn and matrimonially clipped, the Pardoner uses circumcised allegory for uncircumcised ends. The Pardoner figures rhetoric as an emasculated male body.[40] Moreover, in his lack of a clear gender identity, the Pardoner is the overliteralization of—the uncircumcised version of—the Pauline ideal by which "there is neither Jew nor Greek . . . there is neither male nor female" (Gal. 3:28).

Along with the Pardoner's uncircumcision and the glossator's reference to the *praeputium*, the medieval disciplines of theology and medicine also suggest that the male foreskin may serve as a frame of reference for the Wife. The medieval disciplines of theology and medicine both understood the male body as normative and the female body as a deviation from this norm. Through metaphors of circumcision, the male body cleanses itself of physical sin—in a discussion almost synonymous with masculinity.[41] Yet the Wife's deafness links her with the biblical trope of "uncircumcised ears."[42] And, notably, this deafness results from her attempt to literally destroy a text.[43] Moreover, the Wife refers once to her clitoris, which medieval anatomists regarded as equivalent to the foreskin.[44] In other words, there is a kind of queering of the Wife and of the hermeneutic foreskin. The Wife, uncircumcised in body and soul, represents a departure from the ideal articulated by Paul (circumcised in heart and indifferent to the literal penis).[45] In her defiance of Pauline hermeneutics, the Wife (like the Pardoner) flirts with a "Jewish" disposition. In her lustiness, the Wife resembles the (modern) stereotype of the overly masculine Jewish woman.[46]

In addition, the Wife resembles the figure of Synagoga.[47] And, because of her inability to perceive the spiritual meaning of the text, the Wife often references the Old Testament.[48] Also, the Wife blurs the distinction between the Old and the New laws as a central part of the Wife's exegetical strategy.[49] In her status as heretical exegete, the Wife's interest in the "flesh" of marriage—the Hieronymian *praeputium*—bears upon the circumcised/

uncircumcised divide that Paul formulated between Christianity and Juda-ism.[50] Another way to put this: The Wife is the uncircumcision, both textu-ally and matrimonially.[51] In her preference for experience over authority, the Wife seems to develop an allegory out of her own autobiography: She constructs herself as the letter of a text to be read allegorically—as a textual *praeputium*. In her apparel and in her age, and in her identification with the Loathly Lady of her own tale—who turns into a beauty—she embodies the chiastic wit of the transformation of Old into New.

The Pardoner's interruption incites the Wife's extensive discourse.[52] And, notably, the Wife's engagement with patristic theology takes shape in this lengthy preface, which meditates upon the genitals.[53] Taking up the theme of marital fleshiness, the Wife's diatribe assumes the form of an abnormally long prologue. The Friar complains that "this is a long preamble of a tale" (l. 831). Indeed, the Wife's prologue is nearly as long as the General Prologue itself.[54]

I am suggesting that the Wife's Prologue—her preface/prepuce—con-structs her as a kind of textual *praeputium*, as the literal level of textuality that requires circumcising allegoresis. The Wife has—or is—a foreskin. And what I will describe as the circumlogical structure of her Tale works not only to hermeneutically circumcise the Tale itself but also to circumcise this prepuce, that is, the Wife. As the Wife so shrewdly points out, the con-tradictions in Paul's own writings—mainly in his writings on sex and mar-riage—themselves reveal how the body cannot be completely subsumed into allegorical transcendence.

Note, too, the Wife's preference for literal law. Throughout her Prologue, the Wife takes issue with the fact that the theology of marriage does not rest upon what she calls "expres word" (l. 61). The Wife eschews the allegoriz-ing interpretations by which her patristic interlocutors understand mar-riage; she favors instead the plain text. Meanwhile, the Wife subordinates her husbands to what she calls "my lawe"—a rule by which she "governed hem" (l. 219). The Wife favors a kind of literal, fleshly law over allegoresis. Countering Jerome, the Wife resorts to an uncircumcised hermeneutics. As the Wife explains,

> Yet herde I nevere tellen in myn age
> Upon this nombre diffinicioun.
> Men may devyne and glosen, up and doun,

But wel I woot, expres, withoute lye,
God bad us for to wexe and multiplye;
That gentil text kan I wel understonde.
(All my born days, I've never heard as yet
Of any given number or limit,
However folk surmise or interpret.
All I know for sure is, God plainly
Bidden us to increase and multiply—
A noble text, and one I understand!) (ll. 24–29; 150)

Discrediting the diviners, the Wife favors the "gentil text" of Genesis 1:28 ("increase and multiply," etc.).[55] Whereas Jerome used numeric symbolism to force a scriptural interpretation that casts doubt on God's blessing of marriage in Genesis, Augustine developed his understanding of marriage from a plainer reading of Genesis.[56] True. But the Wife does not simply acquiesce to Augustinian hermeneutics. Indeed, her concern for the "gentil text" may even make her the member of a heretical sect.[57]

Against the tradition of working hermeneutically to interpret the flesh of marriage in a spiritual dimension, the Wife, in contrast, cites the "gentil text" without undertaking this kind of interpretive circumcision. The Wife understands "be fruitful and multiply" as a literal commandment to screw and to screw often.[58] By ironically agreeing to the Hieronymic conflation of marriage and uncircumcision, the Wife promotes her own marriages with an uncircumcised reading. For her, the Jewish text becomes Gentile "in the heart" (overly carnal in its literalism).[59]

Her insistence upon the "gentil text" suggests that, in her exegetical approach, she critiques the patristic theories that, using metaphors of circumcision, distinguished between "Jewish" and "Gentile" modes of reading. As a noun, the Middle English "gentil" means both noblemen and non-Jews, and, as an adjective, the word refers to noble rank, gentle character, and to pagans.[60] Christian supersessionary theology transfers the status of the chosen people from Jews to Gentiles, an idea that underwrites the possibility of deconstructing categories of class status.[61]

Also, in reference to Gen. 1:28, the word "gentil" may insinuate the genitals.[62] Given the Wife's abiding interest in the sex organs, and given how the Jew/Gentile dynamic deeply informs the patristic writers with whom the Wife debates, the polyvalent phrase "gentil text" pulses with the chaste *praeputium* of exegesis and with the naughty uncircumcision of the Wife's lust. The Wife construes the act of glossing as a kind of erotic performance, as when she says of a husband that "But in oure bed he was so fresh and gay, / And therwithal so wel coude he me glose" (ll. 508–9).[63] And, as cited previously, the Wife portrays glossing as an "up and down" motion, and she repeats this description later when she discusses the meaning of the genitals:

> Glose whoso wole, and seye bothe up and doune
> That they were maked for purgacion
> Of uryne, and oure bothe thynges smale
> Were eek to knowe a femele from a male,
> And for noon oother cause—say ye no?
> (Twist it how you like and argue up and down
> That they were only made for the emission
> Of urine; that our little differences
> Are there to distinguish between the sexes,
> And for no other reason—who said no?) (ll. 119–23; 153)

Glossing, the Wife says, transpires upon the genitals, and glossers read the genitals through an "up and down" action. This "up and down" motion speaks to Pauline transcendence (to the movement from the "uncircumcised" literal level to the "circumcised" spiritual level). But, because these lines explicitly treat the genitals, the "up and down" motion also performs a masturbatory exercise that exposes the glans of circumlogical meaning. Though authority cannot experience the joys of earthly intercourse, it still strokes the figurative *praeputia* of textuality. The glossers may deny the sexual role of the genitals, but the Wife identifies their glossing as an erotic activity—one that occurs onanistically, within the all-male discipline of theology, or one that occurs heterosexually, as when her husband "reads" her.[64]

When the Wife asserts that Christ "refreshed many a man," and when she jests that, with one husband, she "made of him of the same wode [wood] a croce [cross]," she sees the material elements of Christ's *vita*—his manhood, his cross—as opportunities for commenting wittily on the erotic potential latent in the Incarnation (ll. 146, 485). By mocking the literal level of Scripture—by sexualizing the biography of Christ—she mocks the literary-theoretical *praeputium*. Her own lust for "play" (both sexual and textual) takes place upon the film of her preface/prepuce, which slides up and down between authority and experience, lubricating the friction between spirit and letter.[65]

Her literal text, however "gentil," is exactly the kind of *Gentile* text that needs a circumcising hermeneutics in order to become spiritual. But the Wife refuses to accept the spiritual valence of the text, as though offering a rejoinder to Paul. In her Prologue, the Wife of Bath refers to Saint Paul the Apostle by name or by title six times, more than the Wife directly refers to any other *auctoritee* (ll. 49, 64, 73, 79, 160, 341). In her discussion of Paul, the Wife splits legalistic hairs, pointing out that Paul provided only "conseille" and not "comandement" (ll. 66–67). The Wife insists upon taking Paul as literally as possible—and in this, she offers a challenge to more orthodox Pauline readers, like the Nun's Priest, whose hermeneutic approach is "taketh the fruyt, and lat the chaf be stille" (VII, l. 3441).[66]

As the Wife dwells upon the apparently problematic nature of the female body, she describes how men have constructed women under a Pauline paradigm that distinguishes between inner and outer layers of meaning. In her Prologue, the Wife acknowledges the patristic distinction between spiritual and bodily purity, saying, "Hem lyketh to be clene, body and goost" (l. 97). But, in her Tale, the Wife suggests that misogynists view femininity as unable to acquiesce to this framework. As the Wife explains, misogynists see women as hypocrites (outwardly pure but inwardly impure), and, contradictorily, misogynists also see women as unable to maintain an inner life distinct from outward show. "For be we never so vicious withinne," she explains, "We wol been holden wyse, and clene of sinne" (ll. 943–44; "However faulty we may be within, / We want to be thought wise, and free from sin," 173). Here, women practice the kind of legalism that Paul decries. Yet, as the Wife immediately goes on to say, "Pardee, we women conne nothing hele" (l. 950; "Because we women can keep nothing hidden," 174). Women cannot, that is, hide secrets inwardly. The Wife's jolly body utterly fails the hermeneutic tests outlined by Romans 2. Women are spiritually uncircumcised (outwardly pure but inwardly sinful), yet women are also always outwardly expressive of their interiority (excessively literal). I believe that the narrative process of the Wife's Tale aims to circumcise the female body—to discipline it through allegoresis—in order to liberate it from this double bind.

CIRCUMCISING MARRIAGE IN THE TALE

More specifically, the Wife's Tale constitutes an allegorical representation of the act of *allegorical* reading.[67] In the Prologue, the Wife herself often eschews an allegoresis of Scripture, but she tells her Tale—and the anecdotes in her Prologue—specifically in order to prove a moral point: (ll. 413–14). The Wife's attitude toward story telling borrows from the humanist belief that stories may contain moral truths, and the Wife's heavy garments allegorically represent the veil of allegory that Boccaccio attributes to poetry.[68] Yet the Wife cynically jests about the market value of the edifying moral profit of allegorical fable, as when she claims that "al is for to selle" (l. 414). This pun demonstrates how the Wife sees sex and marriage in economic terms.[69] Like the Pardoner, the Wife tells allegorical stories whose "winnings"—whose moral kernels—are also venal, since they serve her own ends. Indeed, the Wife—in defiance of Macrobius and Augustine—uses a dream-vision allegory in order to propagate her falsehoods (ll. 575–84).[70] The reader cannot trust that this lie is in fact a lie.[71]

Speaking allegorically, the Wife situates her Tale within a pre-Christian past that anticipates a Christian Britain. The Wife describes how, in the days of Arthur, the land was filled with fairies, but friars exorcised these spirits, and now the land is filled with friars (ll. 857–81). The Wife sets up an implicit comparison between the fairies and friars; the "limitours" haunt "every lond and every streem / as thikke as motes in the sonne-beem"—a fantastic image that insinuates a similarity between these friars and the fairies who previously "daunced ful ofte in many a grene mede" (ll. 866–67, 861). Now "ther is noon other incubus but he" (l. 880). By the Wife's time, Christians had replaced pre-Christian antitypes. This world's authority rests upon its interpretation through the present, Christian moment.[72] The Tale, here, is already operating through typology.

This sense of the pagan past—and of its loosely allegorical relationship with the Christian present—seems to inform the Wife's descriptions of the Loathly Lady. Emphatically, the Wife describes the Loathly Lady as old, ancient, and elderly. Such descriptions occur at least sixteen times throughout the Tale, and the Lady's age is a considerable source of her repulsiveness.[73] The Wife holds in contempt all old things, including herself.[74] And it seems to me that a driving force in the Tale is a desire to transform Old into New. Indeed, the Wife shares Paul's interest in reordering the old into the new.[75]

If medieval thinkers sometimes constructed women by analogy with Ecclesia and Synagoga, then, following this line of thinking, the Loathly Lady may function not exactly as a Synagoga figure but as a type that, through supersessionary allegoresis, may undergo a conversion into the "new." The Loathly Lady, in her ability to transform, stands at the crux of the old/new divide, by which circumcision and matrimony are inverse exceptions to covenantal theology. In fact, the Lady practices a form of Pauline exegesis, transforming "old" into "new" and working toward creating a new kind of marriage and gentility.

The Lady intends to teach her husband to understand the spiritual dimensions of marriage. As the Lady herself proclaims, she eschews the material benefits of matrimony:

> For thogh that I be foul and old and pore,
> I nolde for al the metal ne for ore
> That under erthe is grave or lyth above
> But if thy wyf I were, and eek thy love.
> (For though I may be ugly, old and poor,
> I'd not, for all the gold and metal ore
> That's buried under ground, or lies above,
> Be other than your wife, and your true love!) (ll. 1063–66; 176)

Like Hugh and other theologians, the Lady prefers true, spiritual marriage over "office and ese." Notably, the Knight of the Tale is possessed by carnal desires—he is, first of all, a sex criminal, and, in a thoroughly carnal way, he marries for purely fleshly reasons (to save his own hide).

In this way, the Knight resembles Gawain, who protects his own life even at the risk of faithlessness. And, relatedly, the Knight is conspicuously a subject of law—first, because his crime brings him to court; second, because Guinevere's offer of mercy places him within her bond; and third, because he makes a pact with the Lady (a marriage in office without spiritual content). Again and again, the carnal Knight enters into legalistic relationships. It is this legalistic fleshiness that the Lady will convert.

The Lady enables this conversion through her reading of gentility, the tale's moral climax.[76] In her transformation, the Lady reorients her husband's priorities from the material to the spiritual, and, in so doing, she affirms that their marriage rests upon mutual consent (thus making it a spiritual marriage rather than a marriage *ad officium*). At the Tale's climax, the Lady undertakes an allegorizing interpretation of "gentillesse" that precipitates the Knight's conversion. In her reading of gentility, the Lady denies the concept's fleshy aspects in favor of its spiritual dimensions: She performs an allegoresis upon the "gentil" or "Gentile."

Like the category of the "Gentiles" in the works of Paul, "gentilesse" refers to moral as well as genealogical qualities. And the Loathly Lady, like Paul, tries to disentangle these connections through spiritualization. The Wife of Bath's Tale promotes a Boethian view that identifies gentility as a spiritual rather than genealogical characteristic.[77] Certainly the Loathly Lady highlights the theological stakes of Boethian gentility when she cites God as its true originator (ll. 1129, 1162). Whatever the religious origins of the concept, gentilesse undergoes a kind of exegesis: It is read by the Lady in its spiritual rather than material aspects. Moreover, by using forms of the word "gentil" rather excessively (twenty-three times), the Hag italicizes the word, making its meaning not more precise but more expansive.[78] Through excessive repetition—with the word appearing successively, sometimes once per line in consecutive lines—the Lady's speech is witty, slippery and playfully redundant, and allegorizing, perhaps in a spirit of Christian ethics.

The Lady's spiritual interpretation of gentility—like Gawain's post-nick reading of biblical sources—marks the Tale's crucial turn. The transformation of Old into New "cuts" the Tale, rereads the interior of the Lady, realigns marriage with spiritual ends, redeems the Knight, and ends the story.[79] The allegoresis of "gentil" effects a rhetorical circumcision, one that reveals the moral of the text. The Lady's spiritual interpretation of gentility coincides with an act of miraculous, Christian love.

Much as the Green Knight had entrapped Gawain, the Lady has clenched the Knight within a prisoner's dilemma. The Knight faces an impossible choice (like the death that Paul considered the logical conclusion of human moral systems). Like the climactic scene of SGGK, the Lady's turn to allegory enables the Knight's escape from a dire situation.

Now, coming to his spiritual senses, the Knight accedes to allow his wife's sovereignty, and allegoresis takes dermatological form (with the Lady's body radically transforming from old to new). The hermeneutic circumcision that the Loathly Lady performs upon the concept of gentility magically results in the skinning of her own body. Dermatological transformation occasions hermeneutic conversion: The outer layer of textuality undergoes circumcision in order to reveal the inner, allegorical meaning. So, the Wife's

Tale provides an allegorical representation of the act of Pauline allegorical reading.

ALLEGORIZING THE TALE

If the Wife uses marriage to try to generate social change, she uses the structure of spiritual circumcision in trying to accomplish this change.[80] In other words, the Wife's Tale performs a circumcision upon marriage, as part of an effort to use marriage to "think" about self-definition.[81] The Wife engages with a clerical hermeneutic that—rather than simply pointing back to a transcendent, originary moment in the past—is a dialectical process, one in which one transcendent, originary moment (Christ's *vita*) behaves as the mechanism for superseding events antecedent to that moment (the law and history of the Jewish Bible). So, the "authority" that the Wife eschews is not structured in relation to a temporally static past; rather, this authority is committed in principle to a logic of supersession: Clerical authority relies upon an allegoresis that interrelates temporal moments through typology.

Furthermore, and more to the point, this logic of supersession is one of the technologies that the Wife deploys subversively.[82] As part of her project of validating her status in an emerging new order, the Wife in her Tale employs a narrative structure that borrows from patristic circumcising allegoresis. The Wife, like the Church Fathers, rereads the past through allegory. Structurally, her Tale revivifies the present through a recapitulation of the past—and, in this, the Wife is a student of Paul—but her Tale thus produces a vision of marriage not in accord with doctrine. In this way, circumlogical narrative allows the Wife to reimagine marriage—and thereby to reimagine relations between body and community—while her involvement with Pauline allegoresis assuages the rupture.[83]

Of course, how one parses the implications of this argument may depend upon one's perspective.[84] My reading suggests that the Wife uses Pauline exegesis against itself—that, in other words, Pauline textual strategies enable the Wife's claim upon the universal.

THE WIFE AS SIR GAWAIN

Not coincidentally, one analogue of the Wife's Tale features the figure of Gawain. In "The Wedding of Sir Gawain and Dame Ragnelle," Gawain plays a role similar to the one played by the Loathly Lady's Knight. If any continuity of characterization exists between the Gawain of *SGGK* and the Gawain of "The Wedding," then this continuity may embrace the underlying Pauline tension that shapes these plots and that shapes the Wife's Tale. As discussed in my previous chapter, the Gawain of *SGGK* undergoes a circumcising conversion. Similarly, "The Wedding" places Gawain within a legalistic framework—a predicament thrice called a "covenant"—and this legalism becomes transformed not through a converting nick on the neck but through a dermatological miracle that turns the letter of matrimony into a spiritual union (ll. 282, 362, 576). "The Wedding" and *SGGK* represent different attempts to work out the same Pauline problem; *SGGK* concerns itself with the spiritual circumcision of the individual heart, whereas "The Wedding" and the Wife's Tale take up the question of how to spiritually circumcise individuals in their wedded relation to each other.

SGGK condenses the Jewish/Gentile tension upon male bodies, while "The Wedding" and the Wife's Tale project this tension onto earthly marriage. Whereas in *SGGK* male conversion fantastically circumcises textuality, in "The Wedding" and in the Wife's Tale this same fantasy plays out through the spiritual union of husband and wife. Earthly marriage—read by Jerome as a foreskin—works out the implications of a religion theorized by phallic metaphors. In other words, these stories put into practice the theological task of translating marriage from the Old to the New (necessary because of its ambiguous status in covenantal theology) and of translating marriage from the fleshly to the spiritual (necessary because of marriage's sexual component).

Certainly, a different methodological vocabulary might also be used to describe this insight, and reading the Wife of Bath in terms of circumcision may seem somewhat convoluted. But my critical term allows us to see that, however much the Tale engages with the politics of gender, these politics are also structured by—or in analogy with—another cultural system, namely, supersessionary allegoresis. The transposition of the circumcised/uncircumcised dialectic from the male body onto the union of male and female necessarily introduces kinks into the system.

Ideally, the heuristic of Pauline uncircumcision should apply to all humans universally (Gal. 3:28). But, as the Wife reminds us, experience demonstrates that authority's universalism cannot fully spiritualize the genitals. For Paul, the genitals possess no inherent meaning, but, in actual practice (the Wife says) human procreation requires acknowledging some distinction between the sexes. If reading the uncircumcised male body as "circumcised" involves some degree of cognitive dissonance, how much more so to read the union of male and female as preputial—and then to try to spiritualize that union through "circumcision."

So, as "The Wedding" and the Wife's Tale struggle to enact a poetics of circumcision upon marriage, these two poems experiment with strategies for locating the *praeputium* that Jerome identifies with marriage. "The Wedding" manages this issue by diffusing the tension across two characters: It situates Gawain's marriage within Arthur's trial, and the poem thereby dilutes the narrative energy. Chaucer manages this issue by creating the Wife as a frame for the story. The Wife becomes—like the amplified descriptions of Gawain in *SGGK*—the preputial preface to the Tale's circumcising narratology, the carnal text that seems to undergo hermeneutic circumcision.

IMPLICATIONS

While the Wife develops thematic and rhetorical fleshiness through uncircumcised interpretation, the Loathly Lady finally brings spiritual resolution to the Wife's Tale through circumcising allegoresis. The Loathly Lady allegorizes the meaning of gentility in order to excise her husband's carnal concerns and thereby to spiritualize their marriage. The Wife, champion of the uncut flesh, maintains that any Pauline circumcision of marriage must entail granting women access to the allegorical method. The Wife constructs women's sovereignty—rather than human salvation—as the *bona matrimonii*.[85] To the extent that the Wife leverages her circumcising tale to her own, uncircumcised ends, the Wife, like the Pardoner, perverts allegory.

The Wife of Bath, though quite carnal, tells a tale in which she projects this carnality onto the male figure while constructing the female as a force for spiritualization. A certain kind of exegetical cynicism accounts for the many differences between the Wife's Prologue and her Tale. The Wife's romance of transformation does not seem to follow from much of the material in her Prologue.[86] I see these contradictions as similar to the way that the Pardoner's moral fable contradicts his own character. The Wife creates her wittily uncircumcised Tale through a circumlogical poetics, in order that the moral force of Pauline allegory could corroborate her basically un-Pauline theology of marriage. The Prologue and Tale present a dialectic in which the Tale illustrates the conclusion to which the dialectic arrives.[87] My point is that, through the Prologue and the Tale, the Wife constructs a narrative trajectory that builds up her fleshiness and then uses allegoresis as a strategy for trying to persuade her listeners that she has "circumcised" marriage of this fleshiness.[88]

I think that the Tale's concern for "gentility" is particularly suggestive. In the kind of universalizing work that gentility does, gentility echoes the notion of the circumcised heart—an apparently inward, universally human potentiality that is not necessarily raced or sexed or classed, not necessarily housed in a circumcised or circumcisable body. Gentility, as championed by the Hag, is likewise accessible to all. Yet if the "gentile" is allowed to signify, in a punning way, for the genitals—and I don't see why it wouldn't be, given the Wife's fervor for the genitals—then this term is (like the circumcised heart) fleshly and embodied and powerfully interconnected with the sex organs.

But gentility is more gender-neutral than the foreskin, less associated with the male body. And it is not nearly as implicated in the Jewish/Christian dialectic. The Wife's recourse to gentility is, as it were, a logical extension of the Pauline *praeputium*, for, if the concept is not indeed gendered, then it makes some sense to find, finally, a vehicle that is not gendered.

And, in playing deconstructively upon the necessity of the letter, the Wife has used allegoresis to license sex and profit as integral, even, to the office of marriage, from within marriage's allegorized dimension.

Where the circumcision of the foreskin had stood metaphorically for the proper orientation of the spirit, now the gentility of heterosexual marriage stands metaphorically for such a spiritual ordering. The subordination of fleshly particulars and the prioritizing of the transcendent universal had not—even in interpretations of Paul—ever reached a resolution, but, in its dialectical structure, a hermeneutics of circumcision had left enough exegetical wiggle room—enough space between letter and spirit—for the Wife, in her jolly body (and in opposition to patriarchal sexual moralism) to posit her own sense of the spirit, to "cut off," yet again, the "old man" of the law.

CODA

According to one rumor, William Carlos Williams circumcised Ernest Hemingway's first son. At least a half-dozen biographers have disseminated this legend, and I could personally dream of no better way to mythologize Williams's chiseled verse or Hemingway's clipped prose.[1]

But in fact, the story isn't accurate.

Beneath its fictional husk, the fable does contain a kernel of truth. Williams did not actually amputate Bumby Hemingway's prepuce; more precisely, he retracted it. (Williams pulled back the baby's foreskin in order to break the synechia, a tissue that at birth fuses the foreskin and the glans.)

And Williams himself later joined the gossipmongers: He once claimed that reading poetry before an audience felt like pulling "back your foreskin (if you have one) in public." And he bragged to friends that Bumby's retraction had nearly caused Papa Hemingway to faint![2]

Bumby's mythical circumcision—the primal scene of modernism—participates in a long tradition of understanding storytelling in terms of the penile cap. And this has been my theme: Storytellers often embellish facts and stretch the truth. We issue "retractions." And unsympathetic reviewers may sometimes malign us and "cut us off."

I could go on, citing dozens of examples: early modern writers like Jonathan Swift and Daniel Defoe, who attacked their enemies as "uncircumcised"; American luminaries like Ralph Waldo Emerson, who observed that "circumcision is an example of the power of poetry to raise the low and the offensive"; and Herman Melville, who in *Moby-Dick* decked out one of his characters in a whale's foreskin (no joke: The guy wears a foreskin while sermonizing about the Bible).[3]

But besides its literary dimensions, circumcision may be politically foundational, too. If modern political theory could be traced back to an early modern birth, then that early modern birth was quickly followed by a neonatal circumcision.

During the Reformation, Protestants frequently bragged that they had succeeded in "circumcising" Christianity by sheering off the pomp of Catholicism.[4] And Catholics claimed that Protestants were heretical circumcisers.[5] Puritans condemned the Renaissance theater as uncut, and they celebrated their own religious dramas for "amputating the prepuces of the obscene stage."[6] This conflation (of foreskins with the dramatic arts) supplies a crucial subtext to plays like Shakespeare's *Merchant of Venice*, whose antagonist famously plans to cut off a pound of his enemy's flesh.[7]

Later, the trope circulated to describe the development of limited monarchy and constitutional democracy. The seventeenth-century poet Abraham Cowley asserted that the decapitation of King Charles I represented "the Circumcision of the chosen Race." And several writers claimed "both Church and State" were "circumcised" because of the English Civil Wars.[8]

Partisans in the English Civil Wars were known as the "Roundheads" and "Cavaliers." At this point, I probably don't even have to tell you what those words mean now, as slang terms, among British schoolboys.[9]

Arguably, circumcision symbolism is even covenantal for the United States. At least, circumcision symbolism is an important subtext for one founding mythology: The story of how George Washington chopped down his father's cherry tree and, when confronted, "could not tell a lie" and fessed up.

From my Freudian armchair, I have always understood this story as an allegory for Washington's legitimacy as the usurper of patriarchal authority. As the Commander-in-Chief of the Continental Army, Washington had undermined the symbolic Father (King George III) by desecrating the phallic "tree." Having thus called patriarchal authority into question, the story yet seeks to establish Washington's own patriarchal authority (as the "Father of the Country") by emphasizing his impeccable character (he "could not tell a lie").

When I was a kid, I learned that Washington had cut down the tree (a symbolic castration). But in the first known account of the myth, Washington actually only scraped off a little bit of bark.[10]

In 1800, Mason Locke Weems circulated the tale of Washington and the cherry tree, writing that Washington "tried the edge of his hatchet on the body of a beautiful young English cherry-tree." Call me outrageous for seeing this as a circumcision.

But—as Thomas Jefferson would have known from his study of the Roman agriculturalists—Latin writers often referred to the skinned trunk of a tree as "circumcised." And Roman poets likewise euphemized the foreskin as like tree bark.[11]

Weems, moreover, made a point of celebrating George Washington as a kind of Old Testament patriarch:

[Washington] came to the helm in a perilous and fearful season. Like chaos, "in the olden time," our government was "without form and void: and darkness dwelt upon the face of the deep." Enemies innumerable threatened the country, both from within and without, abroad and at home—the people of three continents at daggers drawn with the young republic of America! The pirates of Morocco laying their uncircumcised hands on our rich commerce in the Mediterranean.[12]

Weems, alluding to the opening lines of Genesis, likens Washington to the great I-Am, a circumcising Jehovah who protects the Chosen People from "uncircumcised" pirates.

This, again, is one of the many, dissonant uses of "circumcision." The Barbary Pirates, many of them Muslims, may well have been literally circumcised. But Washington, the spiritual hero of the story, is circumcised in the apparently figurative sense.

Written in high, Miltonic style, Weems's scene borrows from the Bible, in which God had commanded the Israelites to "circumcise" the "foreskins" of young trees (Lev. 19:23).[13] Moreover, the association between tree's bark and Washington's honesty accords with the Augustinian notion of a "circumcision of lies."[14]

Weems's account, in any case, embeds Washington's historical actions within an ethnocentric, circumlogical cosmos—a religiously charmed world in which a spiritual foreskin still covers over earthly reality with the sheen of allegory.

Some say that the world has since become more secular. But in our current political context, debates about circumcision rage on. Although apparently marginal, anticircumcision activists have increasingly brought the foreskin to the fore as an emblem of an identity politics.

In 2011 in California, activists managed to place an initiative on the ballot that would have banned infant circumcision. (The initiative failed.) In 2012 in Germany, a court actually did impose such a ban (later overturned in response to activism by Jews and Muslims). And in 2020, lawmakers in Finland only removed anticircumcision language from a new law after considerable protests.[15]

These activists make a compelling if problematic case. In the United States, circumcision only became mainstream because of a Puritanical fear of sex.[16] But at the same time, some of these activists have produced vicious cultural products (like anti-Jewish comic books and antifeminist memes).[17]

Too close for comfort to the so-called Men's Rights Movement, these pro-prepuce enthusiasts sometimes turn the foreskin into a fascistic fetish.[18]

If, on the one hand, modern liberal democracy agrees that each individual possesses a natural right to bodily integrity and consent, and if, on the other hand, modern liberal democracy agrees that each individual possesses a natural right to raise one's own children, then the foreskin activists have brought the underlying premises of modern liberal democracy into full-blown self-contradiction—the kind of Mutually Assured Destruction that gets decided by a 4–5 vote on the Supreme Court.

To tell you the truth, when I began working on this book, I, too, had opposed circumcision. But to my surprise, my research brought me to a rather different conclusion.

Maybe the persistent power of circumcision symbolism simply follows from the fact that physicality governs how we think. As cognitive linguists have shown, embodiment controls the metaphors that we live by.[19] The terms that we use to think abstractly, in other words, borrow directly from our concrete experience of living in a material world. If the foreskin is a particularly curious body part—always, apparently, slip-slidin' away, perennially prompting the question of whether it even exists—or should exist—and thoroughly charged with spiritual energy—then, no wonder that it continually provides (albeit in patriarchal terms) a vocabulary for imagining the power of poetry to body forth the forms of things unknown.

Meanwhile, as activists have promoted the regrowth of circumcised fore-skins, this idea had inspired my query to think about how a physical skin could be imbricated in temporality.

These tissue-expansion projects draw out the skin so that it will regenerate (on the same principle that the Buddha's heavy earrings had lengthened his lobes). And this distention of the prepuce, tautly pulled in a goal-oriented enterprise, suggested to me the possibility of a mystical *praeputium* aimed toward a transcendent *telos*, a connection with the Augustinian *distentio animi*.

For my own part, I had initially undertaken this project realizing that—as a circumcised white cis-gendered male gay working-class medievalist poet-scholar—my social positionality (and my actual body) may bar me from experiencing, firsthand, certain dimensions of human reality and may further bar me from the culture of my professional studies, the European Middle Ages. In other words, my particular body (the apparatus that I must use to think with) perhaps has somehow trimmed my ability to understand other bodies.

But this is where things get tricky. If I were to assume that only certain bodies can think certain thoughts, then I fall into the trap set by bigots like Luther and Pound, who argued that circumcision "cuts off" some crucial human capacity.

More optimistically, I had set out to see if I could imagine how some little ring of flesh might historically have been interesting to think with (under a Pauline aspect, too, where one could think with the *praeputium* without necessarily possessing a prepuce).

From having considered this material, my own sense is that, however much the foreskin has become medicalized and secular, these ongoing debates about circumcision still empower the tissue as a kind of magical totem for calling into being some essentializing "identity."

It is as if the question—to circumcise or not to circumcise—is still (like in the conflict among the Apostles) a fetishistic mechanism for dictating identity. Whereas in Paul's final reckoning of that conflict, the question itself had needed to be entirely upended.

The terms of the contemporary debate would nominate, in a reactionary way, the foreskin as some charm whose presence must powerfully mark human selfhood, or determine one's integrity as an individual, or stand as the guardian against the violation of one's sacred rights.

In other words, the terms of this debate fail to internalize the more radical claims about human identity made not only by feminists and queers but also by Pauline Catholics.

In my private view (if I may so state it), the very question itself implies, now, a cathexis to the mystifying forces of partisanship and an unwitting assent to the rigid dualistic strictures of white supremacist, cis-hetero-patriarchal, democratic-liberal-individualist, bourgeois-capitalist-imperialist, post-Protestant, secular liberal modernity. With Paul, I want to say, "circumcision is nothing, and uncircumcision is nothing."

If my book could make any contribution to undoing those strictures, I hope, at least, to have done some of the homework that might be necessary before beginning to restore, for further consideration, a traditional (yet cutting-edge) posture from which the contemporary moment has been severed—a medieval way of "circumcising" the soul while not "circumcising" the body, of projecting the self out into an imaginative realm that complicatedly still depends (in its vocabulary) upon the genitals, returning, then, to the world—not only to interpret it, nor merely to change it, but fully to *re*interpret it.

Despite the phallocentric implications of that procedure, it is, for me, compelling as an exercise. The point, on my end, would not be glibly to stand in somebody else's shoes but to realize that, so often, my very basis for thinking might be mired, even, in my own body's normative assumptions (like the fact that I wear shoes or have two feet, which are not universals).[20]

I mean, in effect, that some space might yet exist (call it a *praeputium*, or what you will)—an enfleshed yet extrabodily apprehension—which, if not necessarily itself the means to fuller human communion, may provide a substrate for generating new (and/or old) narrations, poetic forms that regrow our cut-off selves and reenliven our fractured, broken world.

ACKNOWLEDGMENTS

I would like to dedicate this study to my neighbors in New York City. Their hard-earned tax dollars have often supported my teaching and research, and the City University of New York provided a subvention that helped to publish this book.

Please also allow me to thank my friends, teachers, and colleagues, particularly Glenn Burger, Leonard Cassuto, Sarah Chinn, Juan Decastro, James Fuerst, Marlene Hennessy, Eileen A. F. Joy, Wayne Koestenbaum, Scott Korb, Michael Sargent, Henry Shapiro, Arvind Thomas, and Carolyn Vellenga Berman.

I am indebted especially to Steven F. Kruger.

A preliminary sketch of this topic appeared as "Macrobius's Foreskin," *Journal of Medieval and Early Modern Studies* 46, no. 1 (2016). Thanks to the journal's editorial staff and to the issue's editor, Marion Turner.

The present study has benefited considerably from the staff at Fordham University Press, especially Rob Fellman and Eric Newman. And I am deeply grateful for the brilliant guidance of my editor, Will Cerbone, and for the very stimulating criticism of my peer reviewers. Thank you, and thank you for reading!

INTRODUCTION

1. All biblical citations are from the Douay-Rheims translation, by chapter and verse.

2. See Quintilian, *The Orator's Education*, vol. 3: *Books 6–8*, ed. Donald A. Russell (Cambridge, MA: Harvard University Press, 2002), 386; Suetonius, *Lives of the Caesars*, vol. 2: *Lives of Illustrious Men: Grammarians and Rhetoricians; Poets. Lives of Pliny the Elder and Passienus Crispus*, trans. J. C. Rolfe (Cambridge, MA: Harvard University Press, 1914), 428; Pliny the Younger, *Letters*, vol. 1: *Books 1–7*, ed. Betty Radice (Cambridge, MA: Harvard University Press, 1969), 58; and Macrobius, *Saturnalia, apparatu critico instruxit*, ed. James Willis (Leipzig: B. G. Teubner, 1970), 216.

3. See Frederick Mansfield Hodges, "The Ideal Prepuce in Ancient Greece and Rome: Male Genital Aesthetics and Their Relation to Lipodermos, Circumcision, Foreskin Restoration, and the Kynodesme," *Bulletin of the History of Medicine* 75, no. 3 (2001): 375–405.

4. For a theory of conceptual metaphors and their relationship with the body, see George Lakoff and Mark Johnson, *Metaphors We Live By* (Chicago: University of Chicago Press, 1980). For an introduction to medieval understandings of the textual body, see the essays collected in Dolores Warwick Frese, ed., *The Book and the Body* (Notre Dame, IN: University of Notre Dame Press, 1997).

5. I develop this point further in my fourth chapter. See, for now, Saint Ambrose, *Letters*, trans. Sister Mary Melchior Beyenka (Washington, DC: Catholic University of America Press, 1954), 93–96. See also Caroline Walker Bynum, *Wonderful Blood: Theology and Practice in Late Medieval Northern Germany and Beyond* (Philadelphia: University of Pennsylvania Press, 2007), 107.

6. To define forms of wit, Bede cites two of Paul's punning passages on circumcision; see Bede, *Libri II De arte metrica et De Schematibus et Tropis: The Art of Poetry and Rhetoric*, ed. Calvin B. Kendall (Saarbrücken: AQ-Verlag, 1991), 174–75, 196–220. Peter Damian compares urbane, witty speech to a *praeputium*; see Saint Peter Damian, *Die Briefe des Petrus Damiani*, Teil 3, ed. Kurt Reindel (München: Monumenta Germaniae Historica, 1989), 452.

7. See *John Donne: The Critical Heritage*, ed. A. J. Smith (London: Routledge, 1983), 88; and A. W. Barnes, *Post-Closet Masculinities in Early Modern England* (Lewisburg, PA: Bucknell University Press, 2009), 56. Ben Saunders calls this an Augustinian maneuver in *Desiring Donne: Poetry, Sexuality, Interpretation* (Cambridge, MA: Harvard University Press, 2006), 38.

8. See Jim Ellis, "The Wit of Circumcision, the Circumcision of Wit," in *The Wit of Seventeenth-Century Poetry*, ed. Claude J. Summers and Ted-Larry Pebworth

(Columbia: University of Missouri Press, 1995), 62–77; and Robert Herrick, *The Poetical Works of Robert Herrick*, ed. L. C. Martin (Oxford: Clarendon, 1956), 259, 307, 490, 519.

9. Martin Luther, *Reformations Schriften*, Dr. Martin Luthers Sämmtliche Schriften 20, ed. Johann Georg Walch (St. Louis: Concordia, 1890), 1880.

10. D. D. Paige had expunged the relevant passage from *The Letters of Ezra Pound* (New York: New Directions, 1971), 182. Wayne Koestenbaum provides an uncut edition of the letter (based on Paige's unpublished transcription) in "*The Waste Land*: T. S. Eliot's and Ezra Pound's Collaboration on Hysteria," *Twentieth-Century Literature* 34, no. 2 (1988): 113–39, 125. Pound claimed that he had cut off the poem's excesses in order to mark it as male. Koestenbaum, "*Waste Land*," 136. In a letter to William Carlos Williams, Pound also claimed that "someone diagnosed [George Bernard] Shaw years ago by saying he had a tight foreskin / the whole of puritan idiocy is produced by badly built foreskins"; *Pound/Williams: Selected Letters of Ezra Pound and William Carlos Williams*, ed. Hugh Witemeyer (New York: New Directions, 1996), 177.

11. See Arthur P. Urbano, *The Philosophical Life: Biography and the Crafting of Intellectual Identity in Late Antiquity*, Patristic Monograph Series 21 (Washington, DC: Catholic University of America Press, 2013), 122; see also Clement of Alexandria, *The Writings of Clement of Alexandria*, trans. William Wilson (Edinburgh: T&T Clark, 1880), 396–400; and Jaroslav Pelikan, *Christianity and Classical Culture: The Metamorphosis of Natural Theology in the Christian Encounter with Hellenism* (New Haven, CT: Yale University Press, 1993), 32.

12. See David J. Falls, *Nicholas Love's Mirror and Late Medieval Devotio-Literary Culture: Theological Politics and Devotional Practice in Fifteenth-Century England* (New York: Routledge, 2016). Falls points out that Nicholas's *Mirror* diverges somewhat from its source text, the *Meditations*, in its treatment of this scene: "While in the chapter on 'The Circumcision of our Lord Jesus Christ' (Ch. 8), the author of the *Meditations* devotes much of the text to the value of silence, claiming 'we ought to circumcise our tongue, that is, to speak sparingly, and to say only what is useful . . . silence is virtuous, and not without reason a rule in religious orders,' in an almost counterintuitive strategy Love chooses to 'passen ouer' the meditation on the value of silence, commenting only that 'silence is a gret vertue, & for gret cause of gudenes ordeynet in religione, of þe which vertue diuerse clerkes speken þat we shole passen ouer at þis tyme, and þus endiþ þis chaptire'" (36). Falls suggests that this "counter-intuitive" strategy demonstrates how Nicholas wrote the *Mirror* for an audience of Carthusians already accustomed to the silence of the charterhouse. But Falls also suggests that the *Mirror* suits a wide audience, including lay readers (100). Michael G. Sargent has suggested to me in conversation that the circumcision chapter in *The Mirror* marks an important turning point in the narrative: Whereas previously Nicholas had amplified his sources, hereafter he tends to abbreviate them.

13. Bernard of Clairvaux, "In Circumcisione Domini, Sermo I," in *Sermones de*

tempore, de sanctis, de divorsis (Vindobona: Alfred Holder, 1891), 137–41; see also Leo Steinberg, *The Sexuality of Christ in Renaissance Art and in Modern Oblivion* (Chicago: University of Chicago Press, 1996), 54.

14. G. R. Evans discusses this rhetorical play in *Bernard of Clairvaux* (New York: Oxford University Press, 2000), 66.

15. Many references show that, persistently over many centuries, monastic writers have used the trope of circumcision to think not only about how monastic discipline cuts off excesses but also how, more exegetically, this discipline is embedded in a Pauline interpretation of the Bible. See Origen, *Commentary on the Epistle to the Romans, Books 1–5,* trans. Thomas P. Scheck (Washington, DC: Catholic University of America Press, 2001), 146–56; and Elizabeth A. Clark, *Reading Renunciation: Asceticism and Scripture in Early Christianity.* (Princeton, NJ: Princeton University Press, 1999), 226–30. Evagrius Ponticus would have Christians "circumcise the impassioned thoughts in one's thinking"; see Paul Jensen, *Subversive Spirituality: Transforming Mission through the Collapse of Space* (Cambridge: James Clark, 2009), 113. In Ruotger's tenth-century *Life of Bruno,* Ruotger explains that Bruno the Great advocated for a "spiritual circumcision" that would "cut out" a "superfluity of clothes" (apparently as part of the Gorze Reform); qtd. in Henry Mayr-Harting, *Church and Cosmos in Early Ottonian Germany: The View from Cologne* (New York: Oxford University Press, 2007), 41. Peter Damian uses the metaphor to trim off the excesses of the liberal arts; see Peter Godman, *The Silent Masters: Latin Literature and Its Censors in the High Middle Ages* (Princeton, NJ: Princeton University Press, 2000), 28–29. See also Jan M. Ziolkowski and Bridget K. Balint, *A Garland of Satire, Wisdom, and History: Latin Verse from Twelfth-Century France (Carmina Houghtoniensia)* (Cambridge, MA: Harvard University Press, 2007), 88. Ælred of Rievaulx described spiritual circumcision as a complete reorientation of the senses; see Dawn Hadley, *Masculinity in Medieval Europe* (New York: Routledge, 1999), 234. At least one modern monastic writes that what Origen calls the "circumcision of the lips" is precisely the rule of Benedictine silence; see Mark Alan Scott, *At Home with Saint Benedict: Monastery Talks* (Collegeville, MN: Liturgical Press, 2010), 117.

16. For an overview of circumcision symbolism, see Nina E. Livesey, *Circumcision as a Malleable Symbol* (Tübingen: Mohr Siebeck, 2010).

17. Some of these problematics are explicated in Susan A. Handleman, *The Slayers of Moses: The Emergence of Rabbinic Interpretation in Modern Literary Theory* (Albany: SUNY Press, 1982). For uses of circumcision in critical-theoretical approaches to these problematics, see Jacques Derrida, "Shibboleth: For Paul Celan," in *Sovereignties in Question: The Poetics of Paul Celan,* ed. Thomas Dutoit and Outi Pasanen (New York: Fordham University Press, 2005); and "Ulysses Gramophone: Hear Say Yes in Joyce," trans. François Raffoul, in *Derrida and Joyce: Texts and Context,* ed. Andrew J. Mitchell and Sam Slote (Albany: SUNY Press, 2013), 41–86; also see Jacques Lacan, *Le séminaire de Jacques Lacan: L'angoisse* (Paris: Seuil, 2004), 106.

18. See especially Kathleen Biddick, *The Typological Imaginary: Circumcision, Technology, History* (Philadelphia: University of Pennsylvania Press, 2003).

19. In two of her mystical visions, Agnes ate the Holy Prepuce. Agnes relates how she had prayed for a sign to indicate whether she should compose a book of her visions, and she received the Prepuce as just such a sign. The Prepuce licensed Agnes to work in the traditionally male domain of theological writing. Furthermore, Agnes apparently received the Prepuce when she was unable to receive the Eucharist, so that the Prepuce served as a direct channel to the Body of Christ, normally a male prerogative. Although Agnes produced a treatise on her visions, her interest in the Prepuce later resulted in her censorship. With the printing of her book in the eighteenth century, the church condemned Agnes's visions because she implicitly had challenged the orthodox teaching that the Prepuce had remained on earth after Christ's Ascension to heaven. See Ulrike Wiethaus, *Agnes Blannbekin, Viennese Beguine: Life and Revelations* (London: D. S. Brewer, 2002), 10–11, 34–36.

20. The bibliography on this topic cannot expand quickly enough. As the situation develops, I cite Dorothy Kim, *Digital Whiteness and Medieval Studies* (Leeds: ARC Humanities Press, 2019).

21. I follow a model of queer reading through attention to thematic sites advanced by Anna Kłosowska, *Queer Love in the Middle Ages* (New York: Palgrave Macmillan, 2005).

22. On the sexual politics of medieval literary theory, see Carolyn Dinshaw, *Chaucer's Sexual Poetics* (Madison: University of Wisconsin Press, 1989), 23; and Rita Copeland, "Why Women Can't Read," in *Representing Women*, ed. Susan Sage Heinzelman and Zipporah Batshaw Wiseman (Durham, NC: Duke University Press, 1994), 253–86. Arguing that medieval readers understood the textual body as feminine, Copeland (257) and Dinshaw (22) both cite Saint Jerome's Letter LXX, which compares pagan texts to the captive heathen woman discussed in Deuteronomy 21. If marrying the woman is similar to reading pagan literature, I observe that the woman is only marriageable after acts of cutting. According to Deuteronomy, she must shave her head, cut off her eyebrows, and trim her nails; see Jerome, *Nicene and Post-Nicene Fathers, Second Series*, vol. 6, ed. Philip Schaff and Henry Wace (Buffalo, NY: Christian Literature, 1893), 149. Throughout the epistle, Jerome describes textuality by analogy to several other figures, bodies male and female, which also must be cut. Jerome writes that Paul, in citing the Greek dramatist Menander, "cut off the head of the arrogant Goliath" (LXX, 149). And Jerome cites Isaiah and Ezekiel as examples of men who removed their hair in order to make themselves more pious (Isaiah 7:20; Ezekiel 5:1–5; qtd. in Jerome LLX, 149). In my view, Jerome is advocating not for an interpretative penetration but for an interpretative cut.

23. See Mieke Bal, *Narratology: Introduction to the Theory of Narrative* (Toronto: University of Toronto Press, 2009), 3. Generally, medievalists have ignored narratology, and narratologists have ignored the medieval. Evelyn Birge Vitz

observed that classical theories of narrative basically fail to describe medieval nar-ratives: *Medieval Narrative and Modern Narratology: Subjects and Objects of Desire* (New York: New York University Press, 1989), 5. With a handful of exceptions, few narratological studies have addressed medieval narrative, for reasons having to do with both medievalism as a field and narratology as a mode of inquiry. Eva von Contzen attributes this scholarly blindspot to a number of factors, including "the structuralist heritage of narratology, the unsuitability of many existing narrative theories, the bias of the Middle Ages as an inferior period, the lack of medieval-ists invested in narratology, the alterity of medieval literature that poses a problem to non-medievalists, the difficulty of making medievalists' findings available and useful for further narratological studies": "Why We Need a Medieval Narratology," *Diegesis: Interdisziplinäres E-Journal für Erzählforschung* 3, no. H2 (2014). Von Contzen encourages an interdisciplinary study of medieval narrative. In propos-ing that medievalists should undertake narrative studies, von Contzen empha-sizes that narrative patterns order time and space, features that medieval people invested with religious meaning.

I consider medieval narratology in light of theologies of the foreskin in order to begin to apprehend the interrelationship between medieval narrative structure and broader questions of embodiment. In so doing, I make a second contribution to the field of narratology, which tends not to have yet fully explored how narra-tive pertains to the body. Nor have narratologists fully conversed with the lessons of feminism and queer theory. Feminist and queer critics have sometimes applied narratology, but without necessarily addressing issues germane to narratology proper; see Ansgar Nünning, "Surveying Contextualist and Cultural Narratolo-gies: Towards an Outline of Approaches, Concepts, and Potentials," in *Narratol-ogy in the Age of Cross-Disciplinary Narrative Research*, ed. Sandra Heinen and Roy Sommer (New York: Walter de Gruyter, 2009), 48–70, 55. Similarly, Susan S. Lanser sees the need for a queer, feminist narratology: "Toward (a Queerer and) More (Feminist) Narratology," in *Narrative Theory Unbound: Queer and Feminist Interventions*, ed. Robyn Warhol and Susan S. Lanser (Columbus: Ohio State Uni-versity Press, 2015). And toward that end, Judith Roof argues that certain narrative structures enforce heterosexism: *Come as You Are: Sexuality and Narrative* (New York: Columbia University Press, 1996); and Marilyn R. Farwell has investigated the queering of such structures: *Heterosexual Plots and Lesbian Narratives* (New York: New York University Press, 1996).

While I look at representations of the human body—or the body as a repre-sentation—I will examine how this body—messy, constructed, and/or natural—relates to the textual body. Daniel Punday explains that, whereas feminists often focus on representations of the body, they have tended to ignore the body in its relation to narratology: *Narrative Bodies: Toward a Corporeal Narratology* (New York: Palgrave Macmillan, 2003), 6. Investigating eighteenth- and nineteenth-century writing, Punday argues that attitudes toward the body have shaped nar-ratological concepts like character, plot, narration, and setting.

Where scholarship has approached medieval form from a critical feminist perspective, medievalists have focused on the structure of allegory. My own analysis, which understands certain narrative structures as operating allegorically within the framework of Pauline hermeneutics, is an extension of these insights, pioneered by scholars like James J. Paxson, "Personification's Gender," *Rhetorica* 16, no. 2 (1998): 149–79; and Sheila Delany, *Medieval Literary Politics: Shapes of Ideology* (Manchester: Manchester University Press, 1990), esp. chap. 3, "The Politics of Allegory in the Fourteenth Century," 42–60; as well as Noah D. Guynn, *Allegory and Sexual Ethics in the High Middle Ages* (New York: Palgrave Macmillan, 2007); and Simon Gaunt, "Bel Acueil and the Improper Allegory of the Roman de la Rose," *New Medieval Literatures* 2 (1998): 65–93. Queer analysis of medieval rhetorical structures includes A. W. Strouse, "Misogynists as Queers in *Le Livre de la Cité des Dames*," *Romanic Review* 104, nos. 3–4 (2013): 251–71; and David Rollo, *Kiss My Relics: Hermaphroditic Fictions of the Middle Ages* (Chicago: University of Chicago Press, 2011).

24. For the most part, I will cite Latin texts in standard English translations, but when doing especially close analysis will also provide the Latin in notes. Middle English poems I will cite in the original and with translations in-text.

25. Maybe the foreskin is gender dysphoric, as Wayne Koestenbaum intuits in *Notes on Glaze* (Brooklyn: Cabinet Books, 2016), 101. Or, the question of circumcision seems caught up in a concern that either the foreskin is or is not properly masculine: Deciding either to retain or to remove the foreskin, at root, suggests that the skin somehow compromises phallic integrity. Thus various discourses have diverged in coding the skin as feminine, and therefore in need of removal, or as masculine, and therefore in need of retention; see Livesey, *Circumcision*, 50; Leonard B. Glick, *Marked in Your Flesh: Circumcision from Ancient Judea to Modern America* (New York: Oxford University Press, 2005), 105; and Hodges, "The Ideal Prepuce," 379.

1. THE GOSPEL ACCORDING TO THE FORESKIN

1. Elizabeth A. Clark, *Reading Renunciation: Asceticism and Scripture in Early Christianity* (Princeton, NJ: Princeton University Press, 1999), 45.

2. David Gollaher, *Circumcision: A History of the World's Most Controversial Surgery* (New York: Perseus, 2000), 32.

3. Mieke Bal observes that nominalization (forming a noun from a verb) makes a concept analyzable but also obscures the narrative of action and the subjectivities of agents. Note that Bal's example may be triggering but is, I think, quite analogous to circumcision; see *Narratology: Introduction to the Theory of Narrative* (Toronto: University of Toronto Press, 2009), 159.

4. Elliot R. Wolfson, *Circle in the Square: Studies in the Use of Gender in Kabbalistic Symbolism* (Albany: SUNY Press, 1995), 38.

5. Qtd. in Wolfson, *Circle in the Square*, 38.

6. Wolfson, *Circle in the Square*, 38.

7. Oscar Wilde, *The Plays of Oscar Wilde*, vol. 3 (Boston: John W. Luce, 1906), 18–19.

8. "Hellenism [was] symbolized by concealing the glans and practicing infibulation": Waldo E. Sweet, *Sport and Recreation in Ancient Greece: A Sourcebook with Translations* (New York: Oxford University Press, 1987), 133.

9. On Greek masculinity, see David M. Halperin, *One Hundred Years of Homosexuality, and Other Essays on Greek Love* (New York: Routledge, 1990).

10. See Frederick Mansfield Hodges, "The Ideal Prepuce in Ancient Greece and Rome: Male Genital Aesthetics and Their Relation to Lipodermos, Circumcision, Foreskin Restoration, and the Kynodesme," *Bulletin of the History of Medicine* 75, no. 3 (2001): 375–405, 382.

11. Hodges, "The Ideal Prepuce," 382; Felix Bryk, *Circumcision in Man and Woman: Its History, Psychology, and Ethnology* (New York: American Ethnological Press, 1934), 227.

12. "This explanation has the advantage of applying equally to the athletes and the nonathletes portrayed as bound. It even suggests how its appearance in a satyr scene may have functioned as a joke . . . the custom was symbolic of sexual restraint, a virtue often praised in Greek writing, sometimes with particular reference to athletes (see, for instance, Plato *Laws* 839e–40b)." Andrew Lear, "Eros and Greek Sport," in *A Companion to Sport and Spectacle in Greek and Roman Antiquity* (Oxford: Wiley-Blackwell, 2014), 246–58, 255. See also David Sansone, *Greek Athletics and the Genesis of Sport* (Berkeley: University of California Press, 1988), 119ff.; and Elizabeth Abbott, *A History of Celibacy* (New York: Scribner, 1999), 209.

13. See Aristophanes, *Acharnians*, trans. Jeffrey Henderson (Cambridge, MA: Harvard University Press, 1998), 134; *Wealth*, trans. Jeffrey Henderson (Cambridge, MA: Harvard University Press, 2002), 463; and *Birds*, trans. Jeffrey Henderson (Cambridge, MA: Harvard University Press, 2000), 498. See also *Greek Iambic Poetry: From the Seventh to the Fifth Centuries BC* [Hipponax, Archilochus, and Semonides], trans. Douglas E. Gerber (Cambridge, MA: Harvard University Press, 1999), 363.

14. J. N. Adams provides these definitions in *The Latin Sexual Vocabulary* (Baltimore, MD: Johns Hopkins University Press, 1982), 13. Juvenal uses the word in a satire that makes fun of Jews; see *Satires*, trans. Susanna Morton Braund (Cambridge, MA: Harvard University Press, 2004), 466; as does Martial. Peter Schäfer argues that the words demonstrate an imagined similarity between arousal and circumcision in *Judeophobia: Attitudes toward the Jews in the Ancient World* (Cambridge, MA: Harvard University Press, 1997), 101.

15. K. J. Dover, *Greek Homosexuality* (Cambridge, MA: Harvard University Press, 1978), 128–29.

16. Dover, *Greek Homosexuality*, 127–34. Leo Steinberg notes that premodern Christian artists often depicted circumcised biblical figures, like David, with foreskins; see *The Sexuality of Christ in Renaissance Art and in Modern Oblivion* (Chicago: University of Chicago Press, 1996), 167.

17. Constructing the foreskin as an object of courtesy, if not of beauty, Herodotus wrote that the Egyptians "practice circumcision for cleanliness' sake; for they set cleanness above seemliness"; *The Persian Wars*, vol. 1: *Books 1–2*, trans. A. D. Godley (Cambridge, MA: Harvard University Press, 1920), 319.

18. See A. W. Strouse, "Macrobius's Foreskin," *Journal of Medieval and Early Modern Studies* 46, no. 1 (2016): 12–13.

19. See Plato, *Phaedrus*, trans. R. Hackforth (Cambridge: Cambridge University Press, 1972), 247c–d. So, Seneca suggests that the prepuce performs an essential feature of man's condition as an embodied creature. In *Apocolocyntosis*, trans. Michael Heseltine and W. H. D. Rouse (Cambridge, MA: Harvard University Press, 1913), Seneca refers to the transcendent form of the human being as "round, without a head, without a foreskin" (456; "rotundus . . . sine capite, sine praeputio"). In a purely abstract realm, man would exist as a sphere, but on earth, he walks upright and possesses the flesh of his foreskin.

20. Horace, *Satires, Epistles, The Art of Poetry*, trans. H. Rushton Fairclough (Cambridge, MA: Harvard University Press, 1926), 110; Petronius, *Satyricon*, trans. Michael Heseltine and W. H. D. Rouse (Cambridge, MA: Harvard University Press, 1913), 244; Sidonius, *Poems, Letters: Books 1–2*, trans. W. B. Anderson (Cambridge: Harvard University Press, 1936), 278. The Greeks associated circumcision with Egyptians. Note that Aristophanes specifically mocks Egyptian circumcision in *Birds* (498). Herodotus assumed that the "very ancient custom" of circumcision was first practiced among the Colchians, Egyptians, and Ethiopians in *The Persian Wars*, 1:393; Strabo, too, takes the Egyptians as a point of reference for circumcision in *Geography*, vol. 7: *Books 15–16*, trans. Horace Leonard Jones (Cambridge, MA: Harvard University Press, 1930), 339; and Diodorus Siculus implies that Jews learned the practice while in Egypt in *Library of History*, vol. 1: *Books 1–2.34*, trans. C. H. Oldfather (Cambridge, MA: Harvard University Press, 1933), 193.

21. Tacitus, *Histories: Books 4–5. Annals: Books 1–3*, trans. Clifford H. Moore, John Jackson (Cambridge, MA: Harvard University Press, 1931), 182.

22. 1 Macc. 1:60–61; Josephus, *The Jewish War*, vol. 1: *Books 1–2*, trans. H. St. J. Thackeray (Cambridge, MA: Harvard University Press, 1927), 19; and *Jewish Antiquities*, vol. 1: *Books 1–3*, trans. H. St. J. Thackeray (Cambridge, MA: Harvard University Press, 1930), 131.

23. Anon., *Historia Augusta*, vol. 1, trans. David Magie (Cambridge, MA: Harvard University Press, 1921), 44.

24. Martial, *Epigrams*, trans. D. R. Schackleton Bailey (Cambridge, MA: Harvard University Press, 1993), 102.

25. Martial, *Epigrams*, 139.

26. Christian thinkers like Origen emphasized the supremacy of the text's soul over its body; see David Dawson, "Plato's Soul and the Body of the Text in Philo and Origen," in *Interpretation and Allegory: Antiquity to the Modern Period*, ed. John Whitman (Leiden: Brill, 2000), 89–108.

27. Hans Svebakken, *Philo of Alexandria's Exposition of the Tenth Command-*

ment (Atlanta: Society of Biblical Literature, 2012), 81–97. On Philo's circumcision symbolism, see also Nina E. Livesey, *Circumcision as a Malleable Symbol* (Tübingen: Mohr Siebeck, 2010), 47.

28. Philo, *On the Decalogue. On the Special Laws, Books 1–3*, trans. F. H. Colson (Cambridge, MA: Harvard University Press, 1937), 105.

29. Philo, *On the Special Laws*, 277.

30. Philo, *Questions and Answers on Genesis*, trans. Ralph Marcus (Cambridge, MA: Harvard University Press, 1953), 245.

31. Philo, *On the Special Laws*, 104–5.

32. See Philo, *Questions and Answers on Exodus*, trans. Ralph Marcus (Cambridge, MA: Harvard University Press, 1953), 245; *Questions and Answers on Genesis*, 254; *On the Special Laws*, 105.

33. Philo, *On the Confusion of Tongues, On the Migration of Abraham, Who Is The Heir of Divine Things? On Mating with the Preliminary Studies*, trans. F. H. Colson and G. H. Whitaker (Cambridge, MA: Harvard University Press, 1932), 185.

34. See Richard N. Longnecker, *Introducing Romans: Critical Issues in Paul's Most Famous Letter* (Grand Rapids, MI: Eerdmans, 2011), 40–50.

35. As Paula Fredriksen observes, Paul's theology places Christians in "a social no-man's-land" because "in antiquity, only Jews had the legal right to excuse themselves from the cult that normally expressed responsible participation in the life of the city": "Allegory and Reading God's Book: Paul and Augustine on the Destiny of Israel," in *Interpretation and Allegory: Antiquity to the Modern Period*, ed. John Whitman (Leiden: Brill, 2000), 125–52, 129. As Andrew S. Jacobs writes, Jewish circumcision circulated as a mark of Roman power, so that Paul "opts out of this cultural economy of signs" in a way that evades Roman authority: *Christ Circumcised: A Study in Early Christian History and Difference* (Philadelphia: University of Pennsylvania Press, 2012), 11, 24. In addition to the political meanings that circumcision possessed semiotically, the prepuce also functioned in the ancient world as a part of an aesthetic philosophy. Understanding later elaborations of Pauline circumcision as a rhetorical theory requires some background about Greek and Roman beliefs about the male anatomy. Also, Paul received a Jewish tradition that understood the rite of circumcision symbolically and that employed the trope of circumcision figuratively. Matthew Thiessen suggests that first-century Jews did not see circumcision as necessary for converts, so that—practically if not theologically—Paul effectively agrees with at least some Jewish interpretations of the law: *Contesting Conversion: Genealogy, Circumcision, and Identity in Ancient Judaism and Christianity* (New York: Oxford University Press, 2011), 113. Josephus notes the existence of conflicting Jewish views on circumcision in *Jewish Antiquities*, vol. 9: *Book 20*, trans. Louis H. Feldman (Cambridge, MA: Harvard University Press, 1965), 23.

36. See Thiessen, *Contesting Conversion*, 113.

37. As David Gollaher (*Circumcision*, 32) suggests, Paul employed "circumcision" as the epitome of the Old Law, using the term to distinguish between the

figurative and the literal, between what he called the "spirit" and the "letter." And as Paula Fredriksen ("Allegory and Reading," 133) writes, "Paul's association of circumcision with 'flesh' allows him to conflate the physical act urged by his opponents with other 'works of the flesh' which they, too, would doubtless condemn." See also Menahem Kister, "Allegorical Interpretations of Biblical Narratives in Rabbinic Literature, Philo, and Origen: Some Case Studies," in *New Approaches to Biblical Interpretation in Judaism of the Second Temple Period and in Early Christianity*, ed. Gary A. Anderson, Ruth A. Clements, and David Satran (Leiden: Brill, 2013), 133–184, 174.

38. I am indebted to one of my anonymous readers at Fordham University Press for this brilliant line.

39. According to Daniel Boyarin, Paul's allegorical reading of the Law has grave implications, specifically in bodily matters like sex. Boyarin explains that the relationship between Rabbinic Judaism and Hellenistic Judaism (among which Boyarin counts Pauline Christianity) functions dialectically and that "each of these formulations presents cultural ethico-social problems that the other solves . . . more successfully. Thus if Hellenistic Judaisms . . . provide an attractive model of human equality and freedom—'There is no Jew or Greek, no male or female'— they do so at the cost of a severe devaluation of sexuality, procreation, and ethnicity. And if rabbinic Judaism provides a positive orientation to sexual pleasure and ethnic difference, it does so at the cost of determined stratifications of society. A dialectical reading practice puts these two formations into a relation of mutual thesis-antithesis, thus exposing the cultural problems that each answered but the other did not": *A Radical Jew: Paul and the Politics of Identity* (Berkeley: University of California Press, 1994), 231, see also 233. Alain Badiou explains that, for Paul, "it is not that communitarian marking (circumcision, rites, the meticulous observance of the Law) is indefensible or erroneous. It is that the postevental imperative of truth renders the latter indifferent (which is worse). It has no signification, whether positive or negative. Paul is not opposed to circumcision. His rigorous assertion is 'Circumcision is nothing, and uncircumcision is nothing' (Cor. 1.7.19). This assertion is obviously sacrilegious for Judeo-Christians. But note that it is not, for all that, a Gentile-Christian assertion, since uncircumcision acquires no particular value through it, so that it is in no way to be insisted upon": *Saint Paul: The Foundation of Universalism*, trans. Ray Brassier (Stanford, CA: Stanford University Press, 2003), 23.

40. See Kathleen Biddick, *The Typological Imaginary: Circumcision, Technology, History* (Philadelphia: University of Pennsylvania Press, 2003), 6.

41. [Barnabas], "The Epistle of Barnabas," in *The Apostolic Fathers*, vol. 1, ed. and trans. Kirsopp Lake (London: W. Heinemann, 1912), 337–409, 345. Notably, the early-second-century Rabbi El'azar ben 'Azariah cites this same line as evidence that literal uncircumcision is disgraceful—so, he says, "uncircumcision" is used as a metaphor for wickedness, but the Pseudo-Barnabas references Jeremiah to prove that literal circumcision is unimportant because it is trumped by circum-

cision of the heart; Kister, "Allegorical Interpretations," 174. The Pseudo-Barnabas marks out a distinction between the literal and the spiritual, degenerating the former as meaningless while crediting the latter as paramount.

42. David Dawson sees Boyarin's reading as based on "contestable poststructuralist presuppositions": *Christian Figural Reading and the Fashioning of Identity* (Berkeley: University of California Press, 2001), 20.

43. Dawson, *Christian*, 37.

44. Dawson, *Christian*, 38.

45. Dawson, *Christian*, 39. In contrast to the "dualistic hermeneutics" that Boyarin finds in Paul, Westerholm similarly suggests that "circumcision for Paul is a spiritual reality that may or may not assume 'external,' physical forms, forms that are, in their physicality as such, clearly regarded as nonessential to the nature of circumcision." Qtd. in Dawson, *Christian*, 45.

46. Dawson points out that "Boyarin's reading of Paul demands a choice that Paul himself refuses to make: Israel is either a community of physical genealogy or a community of faith" (*Christian*, 23). True. But many Christians later construed Paul as prescribing precisely this disjunction, so that Dawson's recuperative reading of Paul does not adequately credit how receptions of Paul confirm Boyarin's reading. As Boyarin posits, Paul's views on circumcision produced dialectical opposites in the form of rabbinic Judaism and Pauline Christianity, and, as I noted, Boyarin himself would employ a "dialectical reading practice" that resituates these opposites within "a relation of mutual thesis-antithesis." Perhaps, given how Boyarin and Dawson both put forth compelling readings of Paul, this dialectical tension exists within Pauline Christianity itself. In other words, perhaps the post-Pauline antitheses that Boyarin maps onto a Jewish/Christian divide might inhere within Pauline hermeneutics, and perhaps they exist within the Pauline tradition. As Dawson explains, Paul's hermeneutics generated a tension between the figurative and the figural (with "figurative" referring to an allegorical meaning that steers away from literality, and "figural" referring to an allegorical meaning that still preserves literal meaning). "The figurative dimension," Dawson writes, "does not automatically assume a status independent of literal meaning although it always threatens to do so" (*Christian*, 16). Certainly, many readers of Paul have shared Boyarin's view that the letter to the Romans advances a radical form of allegory. Erich Auerbach had argued that "Christian figural reading refuses from the outset the dualism that opens up such a contrast between concrete and abstract, literal and nonliteral"; Auerbach argues that Christian figural interpretation . . . embraces a tension between figurative and figural meaning. Qtd. in Dawson, *Christian*, 16.

47. As Fredriksen has argued in "Allegory and Reading," 140–47.

48. Fredriksen, "Allegory and Reading," 145–46.

49. Fredriksen, "Allegory and Reading," 147.

50. See Eve Kosofsky Sedgwick, *Tendencies* (Durham, NC: Duke University Press, 1993), 8.

51. Judith Butler discusses how an externally performed gender produces the subject's interiority in *Gender Trouble* (New York: Routledge, 1990), 133–34.

52. See Wayne Koestenbaum, "*The Waste Land*: T. S. Eliot's and Ezra Pound's Collaboration on Hysteria," *Twentieth-Century Literature* 34, no. 2 (1988): 136.

53. Koestenbaum, "*The Waste Land*," 136.

54. See Chris A. Miller, "Did Peter's Vision in Acts 10 Pertain to Men or the Menu?" *Bibliotheca Sacra* 159, no. 635 (2002): 302–17; and David B. Woods, "Interpreting Peter's Vision in Acts 10:9–16," *Conspectus* 13 (2012): 171–214.

55. Timothy W. R. Churchill has pointed out that the book of Acts employs a structure that Gérard Genette has called the "repeating narrative." Timothy W. R. Churchill, *Divine Initiative and the Christology of the Damascus Road Encounter* (Eugene, OR: Pickwick, 2010), 225. Gérard Genette defines this as a form "narrating *n* times what happened once": *Narrative Discourse: An Essay in Method*, trans. Jane Lewin (Ithaca, NY: Cornell University Press, 1980), 225–26. As Churchill (107) observes, Acts relates Paul's vision on the road to Damascus three separate times. As Moessner has argued, this structure realizes, at the level of narrative, the message of the Pentecost.

56. Genette, *Narrative Discourse*, 228.

57. Daniel Punday, *Narrative Bodies: Toward a Corporeal Narratology* (New York: Palgrave Macmillan, 2003), 122.

58. Clare K. Rothschild shows how repetition in Acts portrays how "the individual is summoned from a segregating style of Judaism toward a universalizing one": *Luke-Acts and the Rhetoric of History: An Investigation of Early Christian Historiography* (Tübingen: Mohr Siebeck, 2004), 135.

59. Mikhail Bakhtin, attempting to tell the history of how literature assimilates time and space, argued that a particular genre might produce a particular "chronotope" or "time space" in which time "thickens, takes on flesh," and in which "space becomes charged and responsive to the movements of time, plot and history": *The Dialogic Imagination*, trans. Caryl Emerson and Michael Holquist (Austin: University of Texas Press, 1981), 84.

60. Classical rhetorical techniques and Jewish legal procedures inform much of the structure of Acts; see Craig S. Keener, *Acts: An Exegetical Commentary*, vol. 2: *3:1–14:28* (Grand Rapids, MI: Baker, 2013). Also, metanarrations and closed structures have classical precedents; see Tzvetan Todorov, *The Poetics of Prose* (Ithaca, NY: Cornell University Press, 1971), 21, 63.

61. See the encyclopedic overview of biblical repetitions in Leland Ryken, James C. Wilhoit, and Tremper Longman III, eds., *Dictionary of Biblical Imagery* (Downers Grove, IL: InterVarsity, 1998), 720.

62. Joel B. Green suggests that narrative structures in Acts support its interpretative procedures in "Internal Repetition in Luke-Acts: Contemporary Narratology and Lucan Historiography," in *History, Literature, and Society in the Book of Acts*, ed. Ben Witherington III (Cambridge: Cambridge University Press, 1995), 283–99, 284.

63. In Acts 9, Paul receives his revelatory vision, which informs Paul's belief in the superiority of the spirit over the flesh, since Paul knew Christ in the spirit, in contrast to the other Apostles; Boyarin, *A Radical Jew*, 109.

64. Boyarin in *A Radical Jew* claims that Philo, influenced by Platonic thinking, came close to accepting a Pauline universalism that saw Israel as a matter of faith rather than of works (232). In Boyarin's reckoning, Paul, in contrast, insists that circumcision's spiritual meaning alone is important. "Paul went Philo one step further" (234). By understanding Paul's radical treatment of circumcision as figurative, Boyarin constructs Paul as an allegorizer like Philo, and thereby Boyarin aligns Paul with previous readings of the Law and situates Paul within a Hellenized Jewish paradigm. Though Boyarin claims that Paul sees "inner meaning" as trumping the fleshly signs that signify them, Dawson argues that Paul simply locates meaning beyond these signs altogether. Whereas Philo discusses the "inner meaning" of fleshly signs like circumcision, Romans 2 does not refer explicitly to any such "inner meaning." More radically, Paul writes that "neither is that circumcision, which is outward in the flesh," but Paul actually denies that physical circumcision counts as circumcision. Paul's invocation of the inner and the outer, however, lends his treatment of circumcision to the kind of interpretation that Boyarin offers.

2. SAINT AUGUSTINE AND THE BOY WITH THE LONG FORESKIN

1. Here and throughout this chapter, I will cite from *The Literal Meaning of Genesis*, vol. 2: *Books 7–12*, trans. John Hammond Taylor (New York: Newman, 1982), 202. But in this particular passage, I am making two adjustments to Taylor's translation. Note the Latin, as edited in *De Genesi ad litteram libri XII* (Paris: Migne, 1861), 405:

> Fuit item apud nos puer, qui in exordio pubertatis dolorem acerrimum genitalium patiebatur, medicis nequaquam valentibus quid illud esset agnoscere, nisi quod nervus ipse introrsum reconditus erat, ita ut nec praeciso praeputio, quod immoderate longitudine propendebat, apparere potuerit, sed postea vix esset inventus.

Taylor translates *nervus* as "nerve," but *nervus* often refers to the penis, according to Charlton T. Lewis and Charles Short, *A Latin Dictionary* (Oxford: Clarendon, 1879). And I translate the word as "glans" based on its usage in Franz Xaver Schönberger, *Neuestes lateinisch-deutsches und deutsch-lateinisches Hand-Lexikon* (Wien: Sammer, 1842), 219. Given Augustine's overall description, it seems that the boy is suffering from what Galen and even modern doctors would call phimosis, an ailment common in adolescents when the foreskin becomes too tight to be pulled back to expose the head, sometimes causing a discharge.

2. Augustine, *Confessions*, ed. and trans. Carolyn J.-B. Hammond (Cambridge, MA: Harvard University Press, 2014), XI.3. More literally Augustine asks God to circumcise his "inner and outer lips" ("interiora et exteriora labia").

3. See Eugene Vance, *Marvelous Signals: Poetics and Sign Theory in the Middle Ages* (Lincoln: University of Nebraska Press, 1986), 7. Also, Eric Jager has written that Augustine's metaphor gives textuality a bodily aura; see *The Book of the Heart* (Chicago: University of Chicago Press, 1993), 29. And, as Andrea Nightingale notes, Augustine's "metaphorical conflation of the tongue/lips and the penis highlights the bodily basis of human speech": *Once Out of Nature: Augustine on Time and the Body* (Chicago: University of Chicago Press, 2011), 155.

4. Paul's firsthand experiences with circumcision (as a circumcised Jew who himself had circumcised Timothy) are important to Augustine as he tries to understand the nature of honesty and lying. In discussing honesty, Augustine considers accusations that Paul was a hypocrite both in *De mendacio* ("Lying") and in *De opere monachorum* ("The Work of Monks"). See Augustine, *Treatises on Various Subjects* (Washington, DC: Catholic University of America Press, 1952), 63–64, 349.

5. As Taylor observes in his notes on the passage.

6. Augustine, *The Literal Meaning*, 205.

7. "Praeputio, quod immoderate longitudine propendebat": *De Genesi ad litteram libri XII* (Paris: Migne, 1861), 404. Augustine's commentary on Genesis, as the title suggests, strives to understand the book literally (though Augustine very often struggles to stick to his stated agenda). Book XII, which includes the story of the well-endowed boy, deals with visionary experiences and is discussed by Steven Kruger, who compares Augustine's hierarchical system of dream classification to the systems of Macrobius and Calcidius: see *Dreaming in the Middle Ages* (Cambridge: Cambridge University Press, 1992), 36ff.

8. See Vernon Joseph Bourke, *Augustine's Love of Wisdom: An Introspective Philosophy* (West Lafayette, IN: Purdue University Press, 1992), 149.

9. Augustine often uses the word to describe unrestrained lust; see *Confessions* II.5, III.13, IV.25.

10. Augustine, *The Literal Meaning*, 202.

11. Augustine, *The Literal Meaning*, 202–3.

12. Augustine, *City of God*, vol. 5: *Books 16–18.35*, trans. Eva M. Sanford and William M. Green (Cambridge, MA: Harvard University Press, 1965), XVI.XXVI.

13. Elsewhere, Augustine calls the praeputium an "exemplum" that is always easily at hand; see *Anti-Pelagian Works*, trans. Peter Holmes and Robert Ernest Wallis (Grand Rapids, MI: Eerdmans, 1956), 15–78, 3.8.

14. Paula Fredriksen, "Allegory and Reading God's Book: Paul and Augustine on the Destiny of Israel," in *Interpretation and Allegory: Antiquity to the Modern Period*, ed. John Whitman (Leiden: Brill, 2000), 141.

15. Augustine, *The Literal Meaning*, 202.

16. Augustine, *The Literal Meaning*, 202. Note that I have adapted Taylor's translation to show off the participles, according to the Latin: "Vidit quodam die chorum piorum psallentium, laetantium in luce mirabilis; illis ducentibus et

ostendentibus, et felicitates aliorum, aliorumque infelicitatis meritum insinuanti-
bus" (my emphasis). *De Genesi ad litteram libri XII* (Paris: Migne, 1861), 405.

17. Through what Paul Ricoeur has called the *distentio animi*, Augustine posits
time as an expansive "now" in which the mind apprehends past, present, and
future mentally, from the vantage of the present. In *Time and Narrative*, Ricoeur
considers how Augustine's semiotics plays a determining role in his philosophy of
temporality and how Augustinian temporality radically reinterprets the Aristo-
telian plot ordered in terms of beginning, middle, and end. In the *Confessions*, as
Ricoeur explains, Augustine concedes the point of the skeptics, who say that time
cannot exist physically, but Augustine's belief in signs as pointing toward transcendent truth motivates his quest for a spiritual basis for temporality; see the chapter
"The Aporias of the Experience of Time" in Paul Ricoeur, *Time and Narrative*,
trans. Kathleen McLaughlin and David Pellauer (Chicago: University of Chicago
Press, 1984). Augustine's spiritualization of temporality produces a kind of uncor-
poreal theory of plot and human time. Augustine's spiritualization of time—his
theorization of time by reference to the mind rather than to the body—exemplifies
a Pauline sublimation of the body, which in the story is expressed through a
distortion of story over plot. This is similar to what Daniel Punday calls the
"sublimation of the body within modern ways of thinking about plot": *Narrative
Bodies: Toward a Corporeal Narratology* (New York: Palgrave Macmillan, 2003),
104. Augustinian time operates through an interiority that opposes the body yet
resides within the body; Punday writes, "understood as the obverse of the body;
it is what resides within the body, independent of or at least tangentially related
to the events in the material world" (104). Paul's subordination of flesh to spirit
underlies Augustinian sign theory, and in the *Confessions* it also informs how
Augustine conceives of temporality as spiritual rather than physical. This advances
a narrative structure that attempts to transcend the body as a way of making sense
of narrative time. In a sense, Augustine performs a Pauline circumcision upon
narrative temporality.

18. Todorov calls this a temporal distortion; cited in Gérard Genette, *Narrative
Discourse: An Essay in Method,* trans. Jane Lewin (Ithaca, NY: Cornell University
Press, 1980), 29.

19. Augustine, *The Literal Meaning*, 203.

20. John C. Cavadini, in a recent talk on "The Architectonic Plan of Augustine's *City of God*" at the Patristic, Medieval, and Renaissance Conference at
Villanova University, 2019, discussed a passage in *The City of God* that may help
explain Augustine's ambivalence toward the boy's vision. In the *City*, as Cavadini
explicated, Augustine takes issue with the Roman civic cult and furthermore with
Varro's allegoresis of the underlying pagan myths. According to Cavadini, Varro's
allegoresis produces not a theology but an ideology, "reducing both myth and men
to the status of mere signifiers, bearers of a signification supplied, after the fact. . . .
The human being is left over as the byproduct of signification, as wreckage and

trash, sacrificed by the natural theology to justify the cults by making them appear rational, rather than political." It may be that Augustine is uncomfortable with the boy's visions for similar reasons.

21. Augustine, *The Literal Meaning*, 203.

22. See "In Answer to the Jews," in *Treatises on Marriage and Other Subjects*, ed. Roy J. Deferrari (Washington, DC: Catholic University of America Press, 1955), 393.

23. As Fredriksen ("Allegory and Reading," 143) writes, Augustine's "view of the Law as constant, God-given and good both before and after the coming of Christ affects the tone of his typologies: if the Old Testament is the concealed form of the New and vice versa, then they are each alike in dignity and positive religious value." Thus Augustine advanced principles of exegesis that "brought him . . . much closer to some of the historical Paul's fundamental positions than were many of the theologians standing between them" (148).

24. This is not said explicitly by Augustine but seems to be the most likely conjecture. Given Taylor's position that the boy was "among us" in the sense that he belonged to Augustine's monastic community, the boy's backsliding suggests that he left the community, for "he did not remain steadfast in his pursuit of sanctity." Augustine, *The Literal Meaning*, 203.

25. "The soul," Foucault had said, "is the prison of the body": *Discipline and Punish: The Birth of the Prison*, trans. Alan Sheridan (New York: Vintage, 1995), 30.

26. See Virginia Burrus, Mark D. Jordan, and Karmen MacKendrick, *Seducing Augustine: Bodies, Desires, Confessions* (New York: Fordham University Press, 2010), 93–98.

27. See Jacob Press, "You Go, Figure: or, The Rape of a Tripe in the 'Prioress's Tale,'" in *Queer Theory and the Jewish Question*, ed. Daniel Boyarin, Daniel Itzkovitz, and Ann Pellegrini (New York: Columbia University Press, 2003), 285–310.

3. NICKING SIR GAWAIN

1. I cite *SGGK* from Malcolm Andrew and Ronald Waldron, *The Poems of the Pearl Manuscript: Pearl, Cleanness, Patience, Sir Gawain and the Green Knight* (Berkeley: University of California Press, 1978), giving in-text citations with line numbers from this edition. I also provide parenthetically a translation by the same authors, *The Poems of the Pearl Manuscript in Modern English Prose: Pearl, Cleanness, Patience, Sir Gawain and the Green Knight* (Liverpool: Liverpool University Press, 2013).

2. In Geraldine Heng's reading of *Sir Gawain and the Green Knight*, the "features of the feminine body come to carry a special rhetorical valence, functioning, like the elements of language, on multiple registers of persuasion: one might say, without exaggeration, that the body here is structured like, and actively structures, a language": "A Woman Wants: The Lady, *Gawain*, and the Forms of Seduction," *Yale Journal of Criticism* 5, no. 3 (1992): 101–34, 109. Amitai Aviram puts the same principle into more general and more formalist terms: Aviram writes that a

poem's content can "indicate something that itself cannot be brought into speech directly—the physical experience of the sublime power of sound and rhythm": *Telling Rhythm: Body and Meaning in Poetry* (Ann Arbor: University of Michigan Press, 1994), 24.

3. Undoubtedly, *SGGK* takes a strong interest in circumcision. Henry L. Savage has pointed out that Gawain's adventures begin and end on the Feast of the Circumcision and suggests that the *Officium Circumcisionis* saturates the poem. As Savage puts it, "the poet's eye was glued to the liturgical calendar": *The Gawain-Poet: Studies in His Personality and Background* (Chapel Hill: University of North Carolina Press, 1956), 538ff. Hans Schnyder likewise asserted that the poem's engagement with circumcision resonates even for those modern readers who possess little knowledge of circumcision's allegorical meaning: *Sir Gawain and the Green Knight: An Essay in Interpretation* (Bern: Francke Verlag, 1961), 44. Prompted by Morton Bloomfield, later scholars took a greater interest in the specifically Christian elements; see Donald R. Howard, "Sir Gawain and the Green Knight," in *Recent Middle English Scholarship and Criticism: Survey and Desiderata*, ed. J. Burke Severs (Pittsburgh, PA: Duquesne University Press, 1971), 29–54, 34. Bernard S. Levy regards Gawain's ordeal as a "spiritual circumcision." Qtd. in Howard, "Sir Gawain," 35. John Gardner sees patristic thinking as central to the poem, and Lynn Staley Johnson sees medieval homiletic interpretations of Christ's Circumcision as key to *SGGK*. Qtd. in Howard, "Sir Gawain," 35, 64. Similarly, Wendy Clein reads the poem in relation to John Mirk's sermon for the Feast of the Circumcision, which meditates on how one must "kytte away from hym þe lust of his flesche and worldes lykyng": *Concepts of Chivalry in Sir Gawain and the Green Knight* (Norman, OK: Pilgrim Books, 1987), 61. Clein sees such sermons as underlying a chivalric defiance of death (58). Victor Yelverton Haines also comments on "the symbolic death of the circumcision nick on the Feast of the Circumcision . . . followed by new life in a new year": *The Fortunate Fall of Sir Gawain: The Typology of Sir Gawain and the Green Knight* (Washington, DC: University Press of America, 1982), 104. R. A. Shoaf argues that circumcision grounds the poem's reflections on medieval political economy: *The Poem as Green Girdle: Commercium in Sir Gawain and the Green Knight* (Gainesville: University Press of Florida, 1984), 3ff. Piotr Sadowski suggests that the poem echoes those societies in which circumcision subordinates the sexual drive and marks a boy's entry into manhood: *The Knight on His Quest: Symbolic Patterns of Transition in Sir Gawain and the Green Knight* (Newark: University of Delaware Press, 1996), 211. And Norman Toby Simms audaciously asserts that the poem's "bloody sexuality" demonstrates its suitability for an audience of conversos: *Sir Gawain and the Knight of the Green Chapel* (Lanham, MD: University Press of America, 2002), 63.

4. For a discussion of authorship, see Andrew and Waldron, *The Poems of the Pearl Manuscript*, 16.

5. Sarah McNamer sees the extravagant structure of *Pearl* as indicative of a courtly audience: "The Literariness of Literature and the History of Emotion,"

PMLA 130, no. 5 (2015): 1433–42, 1438. In Morton W. Bloomfield's estimation, "The love of decorative detail in *Gawain* and much of the poetry of the period is probably a reflex of the idea of courtesy and chivalric manners": "Sir Gawain and the Green Knight: An Appraisal," *PMLA* 76, no. 1 (1961): 7–19, 11.

6. A stock alliterative line, "stif and stronge" also describes the plaint of the birds in *The Owl and the Nightingale*, ed. Neil Cartlidge (Exeter: University of Exeter Press, 2001), l. 5. But that particular debate also becomes "softe" (l. 6). Forms of the word "stif" describe masculine qualities in lines 1614 and 2099. Robert of Gloucester uses the phrase "stif mon" in *The Metrical Chronicle of Robert of Gloucester*, vol. 2, ed. William Aldis Wright (Cambridge: Cambridge University Press, 2012), l. 7732.

7. As noted in Marie Borroff, "Systematic Sound Symbolism in the Long Alliterative Lines of *Beowulf* and *Sir Gawain*," in *English Historical Metrics*, ed. C. B. McCully and J. J. Anderson (New York: Cambridge University Press, 1996), 120–33, 120.

8. Catherine Batt, "Gawain's Antifeminist Rant, the Pentangle, and Narrative Space," *Yearbook of English Studies* 22 (1992): 117–39, 120; Geoffrey Shepherd, "The Nature of Alliterative Poetry in Late Medieval England," *Proceedings of the British Academy* 56 (1970): 57–76, 59.

9. For an analysis of ll. 16–19, see Adrien Bonjour, "Werre and wrake and wonder ('Sir Gawain', 1.16)," *English Studies: A Journal of English Language and Literature* 32 (1951): 70–72. Note that the word "burn" might generically mean "a human being," but it primarily means "a man" or "male person," and it often refers to soldiers or knights—a meaning suggested by the context (*MED*).

10. See Jeffrey Jerome Cohen, *Of Giants: Sex, Monsters, and the Middle Ages* (Minneapolis: University of Minnesota Press, 1999), 150. With a pronounced ambivalence toward masculinity, the first fitt of *SGGK* offers a challenge to those critics who would use the poem as an instrument for the deconstruction of contemporary categories of gender and sexuality. In order to develop such an argument, critics have imagined that the poem advances some form of gender essentialism. Carolyn Dinshaw writes, for example, that the Gawain poet believes in a "straight gender," which Dinshaw reveals as riddled with aporias: "A Kiss Is Just a Kiss: Heterosexuality and Its Consolations in Sir Gawain and the Green Knight," *Diacritics* 24, nos. 2–3 (1994): 205–26, 214. But, as Derek Brewer points out, Gawain achieves a kind of maturity without relying on a heroine: *Symbolic Stories: Traditional Narratives of the Family Drama* (Totowa, NJ: Rowman & Littlefield, 1980), 72. Brewer recognized the poem's protagonist as a heterogeneous psyche vexed by Oedipal struggles. Brewer saw *SGGK* as the story of the archaic "conflict between the protagonist and his parents": "Escape from the Mimetic Fallacy," in *Studies in Medieval English Romances: Some New Approaches*, ed. Derek Brewer (Cambridge: D. S. Brewer, 1988), 1–10, 8. Geraldine Heng contends that Brewer engaged in "a homogenizing of the text": "Feminine Knots and the Other Sir Gawain and the Green Knight," *PMLA* 106, no. 3 (1991): 500–14, 500. But Brewer's analysis does

not aim to erase women from the work or to flatten the poem with a totalizing interpretation; rather, Brewer locates the poem's central conflict within the male ego, reading *SGGK* through a theory of the folktale that emphasized the inner conflicts of a tale's protagonist. Although this approach has gone out of fashion, it does not fundamentally disagree with the positions taken by Heng or Dinshaw about the basically heterogeneous nature of sexuality, gender, and textuality: Instead, the difference in approach lies in where critics have located conflict. Whereas Dinshaw and Heng argue that the poet intends to construct a straight masculinity and then fails in this effort, I concur with readers like Cohen and Brewer, who hold that the poet himself accepts as given the futility in such a project. As Bloomfield explained, the "moral elements in the poem . . . are obvious from beginning to end" ("Sir Gawain," 14). Bloomfield understood these moral elements as specifically Christian, and elsewhere in the manuscript the poet identifies "traysoun and trichcheryre" as well as "resounes untrwe" as sins that naturally follow from man's fallen status (*Cleanness*, ll. 187, 184).

11. As discussed in Thomas Stehling, "To Love a Medieval Boy," in *Literary Visions of Homosexuality*, ed. Stuart Kellogg (New York: Haworth, 1983), 151–70, 157.

12. Steven F. Kruger points out in conversation that these conventions do not necessarily apply in the French romance tradition.

13. In a sense, Arthur has trumped Morgan le Fay, since Arthur commands the poem that contains Morgan's games.

14. As Thorlac Turville-Petre notes, the wheels are used "to round off a particular stage in the narrative by summing up or by generalising upon what has been described in the preceding unrhymed lines": *The Alliterative Revival* (Cambridge: D. S. Brewer, 1977), 62.

15. In Cotton Nero A.x., the scribe carefully distinguishes between the main strophe and the wheel by offsetting the bob from the main text; see Israel Gollancz, ed., *Pearl, Cleanness, Patience, and Sir Gawain, Reproduced in Facsimile from the Unique MS. Cotton Nero A.x in the British Museum*, EETS 162 (London: Oxford University Press, 1923).

16. Saint Ambrose, *Letters*, trans. Sister Mary Melchior Beyenka (Washington, DC: Catholic University of America Press, 1954), 96, 95, 93. See also Caroline Walker Bynum, *Wonderful Blood: Theology and Practice in Late Medieval Northern Germany and Beyond* (Philadelphia: University of Pennsylvania Press, 2007), 107. Christ himself, according to some readers of the Book of John, spoke of literal circumcision as the prefiguration of salvation. When criticized for healing a man on the Sabbath, Christ asked his accusers, "If a man receive circumcision on the Sabbath day, that the law of Moses may not be broken; are you angry at me because I have healed the whole man on the Sabbath day?" (John 7:23). As Severino Pancaro points out, Christ refers to the mark of the covenant as a precedent, making circumcision a means to measure past and present: "in the sense that circumcision was—like all Jewish rites and like Judaism itself—but the shadow of things to come. The Jewish rite of initiation, which made man a member of God's

people, was unable to give man what Jesus came to bring. Jesus alone gives men the power to become children of God and to have life in abundance, and this is what was prefigured by circumcision": *The Law in the Fourth Gospel: The Torah and the Gospel, Moses and Jesus, Judaism and Christianity According to John* (Leiden: Brill, 1975), 165. Christ elaborates from the prepuce to the "whole man" and amplifies "circumcision" into a parable for salvation. In this Gospel anecdote, the foreskin stands as the synecdoche that enables allegorical thinking—the parable itself, even—to collapse the Old into the New. As Pancaro notes, this formulation has a temporal dimension. The past of the literal Law represents, in its essence, the present of the spiritual. Circumcision binds old and new. Justin Martyr likewise wrote that "the precept of circumcision . . . was a type of the true circumcision by which we are circumcised from error and wickedness through our Lord Jesus Christ." Qtd. in Leo Steinberg, *The Sexuality of Christ in Renaissance Art and in Modern Oblivion* (Chicago: University of Chicago Press, 1996), 164. Craig D. Allert explains that, in Justin's theology, "circumcision is presented as representing the entire discussion on the Jewish rites which preceded": *Revelation, Truth, Canon, and Interpretation: Studies in Justin Martyr's Dialogue with Trypho* (Leiden: Brill, 2002), 56. Through spiritualized circumcision, Christianity supersedes what Augustine called the "Old Man" of Scripture. The "prae-putium" of the Old Testament intimates the New.

17. Gregory Adams and Kristina Adams, "Circumcision in the Early Christian Church: The Controversy That Shaped a Continent," in *Surgical Guide to Circumcision*, ed. David A. Bolnick, Martin Koyle, and Assaf Yosha (London: Springer-Verlag, 2012), 291–98, 291.

18. John W. O'Malley, discussing sacred oratory of the late Middle Ages, writes that homilists tended to read all events in the life of Christ as an extension or reflection of the Incarnation and as having redemptive value, so that "the shedding of the blood at the Circumcision adumbrates the Crucifixion," and, similarly, "the Resurrection and the Ascension fuse in their specific redemptive effects": *Praise and Blame in Renaissance Rome: Rhetoric, Doctrine, and Reform in the Sacred Orators of the Papal Court, 1450–1521* (Durham, NC: Duke University Press, 1979), 142. Allegorical reading tends to collapse each moment of Christ's life into the same soteriological scheme.

19. As Shoaf has pointed out in *The Poem as Green Girdle*, 20. Whereas Shoaf understands the "exchange" in commercial terms, I am more interested in the exchange as an exegetical translation of literal to figurative.

20. Hymns for the Feast of the Circumcision specifically foreground the allegorical nature of the holiday, for example:

Salvatoris hodie
    Sanguis praegustatur
In quo Sion filiae
    Stola candidatur.

(Today is foretasted the Savior's blood, in which the tunic of the daughter of Zion is laundered).

G. M. Dreves, C. Blume, and H. M. Bannister, eds., *Analecta hymnica medii aevi* (Leipzig: Fues's Verlag, 1854–1919), 20.132; my translation. As the outer veil of foreskin morphs into the laundered, outer veil of tunic, this translation from "literal" to "figurative" also entails a transition from the (ostensibly) male foreskin to the (ostensibly) feminine tunic.

For other examples, see "In Circumcisione DN," in Dreves et al., *Analecta*, 8.16; "In purificatione BMV," in Dreves et al., *Analecta*, 4.54; "De sancto Johanne Baptista," in Dreves et al., *Analecta*, 3.48; "In Circumcision Domini," in Dreves et al., *Analecta*, 39.52; Louis Coutier Biggs, ed., *Hymns Ancient and Modern* (London: Novello, 1867), 69, 71; John Chandler, *The Hymns of the Primitive Church* (London: John W. Parker, 1837), 179. See also Antonio Lollio, *Oratio circumcisionis dominicae* (Rome: S. Plannck, 1485); the discussion of the sermon in Leonard B. Glick, *Marked in Your Flesh: Circumcision from Ancient Judea to Modern America* (New York: Oxford University Press, 2005), 95; Steinberg, *The Sexuality of Christ*, 172, 62; Gabriel Harvey, *The Works of Gabriel Harvey*, ed. Alexander Bulloch Grosart (New York: AMS Press, 1966), 93; William Cartwright, *The Life and Poems of William Cartwright*, ed. R. Cullis Goffin (Cambridge: Cambridge University Press, 1918), 139; and Richard Crashaw, *The Poems of Richard Crashaw*, ed. L. C. Martin (Oxford: Clarendon, 1957).

21. See Robert Herrick, *The Poetical Works of Robert Herrick*, ed. L. C. Martin (Oxford: Clarendon, 1956).

22. See Joannes Bollandus, ed., *Acta sanctorum*, vol. 1 (Paris: Victor Palmé, 1866), 2–3.

23. See Steinberg, *The Sexuality of Christ*, 172.

24. As suggested in W. A. Davenport, *The Art of the Gawain-Poet* (London: Athlone, 1978), 39–41.

25. Davenport, *The Art of the Gawain-Poet*, 141.

26. Davenport, *The Art of the Gawain-Poet*, 143.

27. Davenport, *The Art of the Gawain-Poet*, 154.

28. Such tautological formations occur often in Middle English alliterative verse; see G. A. Lester, *The Language of Old and Middle English Poetry* (New York: St. Martin's, 1996), 128–29.

29. In *Cleanness*, God creates what he calls a "forwarde" with Noah (l. 327).

30. In the contemporaneous alliterative poem *Piers Plowman*, the poet discusses the interpretation of the "nudum ius" ("naked law"); William Langland, *Piers Plowman: A Parallel-Text Edition of the A, B, C, and Z Versions*, vol. 1, ed. A. V. C. Schmidt (New York: Longman, 1995), B. Prol., l. 135.

31. See Richard Zeikowitz, "Befriending the Medieval Queer: A Pedagogy for Literature Classes," *College English* 65, no. 1 (Special Issue: "Lesbian and Gay Studies/Queer Pedagogies") (2002): 67–80.

32. "The poem makes this clear in its frequent association of Gawain's virtues with his items of clothing." Cecilia A. Hatt, *God and the Gawain-Poet: Theology and Genre in "Pearl," "Cleanness," "Patience," and "Sir Gawain and the Green Knight"* (Rochester: D. S. Brewer, 2015), 194.

33. Stephanie Hollis argues that "he appears to wear his distinguishing identity, which is equivalent to his reputation, as an extraneous adornment": "The Pentangle Knight: *Sir Gawain and the Green Knight*," *Chaucer Review* 15 (1981): 267–81, 273.

34. Hollis ("The Pentangle Knight," 193) refers to these amplified descriptions as instances of "the vain attempt to enclose, to find safety in appropriate places." As Hatt (*God and the Gawain-Poet*, 194) puts it, "Gawain surrounds himself with shielding devices of one sort or another, to deal with both moral and physical attacks."

35. As Sarah Stanbury has argued, the *Gawain*-Poet's interest in architectural enclosures should be read in relation to contemporary images of the body as a castle: "Space and Visual Hermeneutics in the 'Gawain'-Poet," *Chaucer Review* 21, no. 4 (1987): 476–89, 477.

36. See John Speirs, "Sir Gawain and the Green Knight," *Scrutiny* 16 (1949): 274–300, 287.

37. Simms, *Sir Gawain and the Knight of the Green Chapel*, 383.

38. J. J. Anderson, ed., *Sir Gawain and the Green Knight, Pearl, Cleanness, Patience* (London: J. M. Dent, 1996), 309.

39. Heng ("Feminine Knots," 503) describes the "feminine text" or "feminine knot" as "an interlinked, overlapping tracery, culminating in a pattern not unlike the familiar one invoked in the pentangle . . . a knot of the feminine and the figure of another desire and its text."

40. As William Perry Marvin explains, the narrative technique of fitt 3, which alternates between the view of Gawain's seduction and the killing and butchering of animals, reproduces the hunter's strategy of chopping up bodies in order to reshape unities: *Hunting Law and Ritual in Medieval English Literature* (Rochester, NY: D. S. Brewer, 2006), 149.

41. This is Biddick's vocabulary. Kathleen Biddick, *The Typological Imaginary: Circumcision, Technology, History* (Philadelphia: University of Pennsylvania Press, 2003).

42. Eugene Vinaver discusses how, in using techniques of interlacing, romances resemble Romanesque design patterns: *The Rise of Romance* (New York: Oxford University Press, 1971), 78–79.

43. Henry L. Savage, using evidence garnered from hunting treatises and from heraldry, has explained in great detail the close degree of correspondence between Gawain's seduction and the hunting of the beasts: "The Significance of the Hunting Scenes in Sir Gawain and the Green Knight," *Journal of English and Germanic Philology* 27, no. 1 (1928): 1–15, 6–7.

44. Muriel Ingham and Lawrence Barkley, "Further Animal Parallels in 'Sir Gawain and the Green Knight,'" *Chaucer Review* 13, no. 4 (1979): 384–86, 386.

45. David Rosen, *The Changing Fictions of Masculinity* (Chicago: University of Illinois Press, 1993), 33–34.

46. For the view that no "symbolic parallel" exists between the hunting scenes and the seduction scenes, see J. R. R. Tolkien and E. V. Gordon, *Sir Gawain and the Green Knight*, 2nd ed., ed. Norman Davis (New York: Oxford University Press, 1967), 107. Indeed, from a certain vantage, the ascribed symbolic parallels do not exist. Or, they become clear only from a retrospective vantage. As Davenport shows—and as I previously mentioned—the poem's structure encourages the reader to produce initial interpretations and then to revise them later.

47. See Savage, "The Significance," 1.

48. Brewer (*Symbolic Stories*, 81) calls the Exchange of Winnings a "witty structural pun."

49. Heng, "A Woman Wants," 108.

50. See C. Clark, "Sir Gawain and the Green Knight: Characterisation by Syntax," *Essays in Criticism* 16, no. 4 (1966): 361–74.

51. Heng, "A Woman Wants," 104.

52. A. T. E. Matonis, "Non-*aa/ax* Patterns in Middle English Alliterative Long-Line Verse," in *English Historical Metrics*, ed. C. B. McCully and J. J. Anderson (New York: Cambridge University Press, 1996), 134–49, 146–48.

53. As theorized by Dinshaw, Copeland, and Heng.

54. As Marvin (*Hunting Law*, 132) puts it: "In *Sir Gawain*, the 'ritual' of slaughter ostensibly contains the violence it conjures forth by sublimating it through customs of venery, but its interlacing with erotic fantasy unravels that containment by letting the action drift as close to violate dissolution as it can."

55. Marvin, *Hunting Law*, 147–48.

56. Marvin, *Hunting Law*, 157.

57. Priscilla Martin notes that, while all four of the *Gawain* poems "insist on allegorical, symbolic, or analogic understanding," most critics have found that these poems "are not consistently allegorical narratives": "Allegory and Symbolism," in *A Companion to the Gawain Poet*, ed. Derek Brewer and Jonathan Gibson (Cambridge: D. S. Brewer, 1997), 315–28, 316.

58. Spearing and Davenport both asserted that the *Gawain*-Poet, more than many of his contemporaries, took an interest in the literal texture of Scripture. Qtd. in Martin, "Allegory and Symbolism," 316.

59. Richard Newhauser, "Scriptural and Devotional Sources," in *A Companion to the Gawain Poet*, ed. Derek Brewer and Jonathan Gibson (Cambridge: D. S. Brewer, 1997), 257–76, 270.

60. Batt, "Gawain's Antifeminist Rant," 137.

61. Gerald Morgan, "Medieval Misogyny and Gawain's Outburst against Women in 'Sir Gawain and the Green Knight,'" *Modern Language Review* 97, no. 2 (2002): 265–78, 277.

62. Again, drawing on the thesis of Biddick, *The Typological Imaginary*.

63. Geoffrey Chaucer, *The Riverside Chaucer*, ed. Larry D. Benson (New York:

Houghton Mifflin, 1987), 5.1865. On the history of this patristic formulation and its transmission to Chaucer through Dante and Boccaccio, see John S. P. Tatlock, "*Purgatorio* XI. 2–3 and *Paradiso* XIV. 30," *Romanic Review* 10 (1919): 274–76.

64. Giovanni Boccaccio, *Boccaccio on Poetry*, ed. Charles G. Osgood (New York: Liberal Arts Press, 1956), 53. For a discussion of Middle English poetry and its relationship with humanist literary theory, see A. C. Spearing, *Medieval to Renaissance in English Poetry* (Cambridge: Cambridge University Press, 1985), chap. 1–2.

65. Shaye J. D. Cohen, *Why Aren't Jewish Women Circumcised? Gender and Covenant in Judaism* (Berkeley: University of California Press, 2005), 10–11.

66. Other Middle English sources likewise describe God's agreement with Noah in the same covenantal language. In the Chester pageant of *Noah's Flood*, for example, God proclaims: "forwarde, Noe, with thee I make" (l. 301).

67. My agenda is not so much to historicize trends in lay piety; rather, I mean to establish how the *Gawain* poems translate the ancient tradition of spiritual purity. As Nicholas Watson explains, "*Pearl, Cleanness*, and *Patience* represent a sustained attempt to translate an ancient tradition of thought concerning the centrality of purity in the Christian life—a tradition going back at least to the virginity literature of the fourth and early fifth centuries—from its old context in monastic and anchoritic writing to address the needs and aspirations of a lay elite": "The *Gawain*-Poet as a Vernacular Theologian," in *A Companion to the Gawain Poet*, ed. Derek Brewer and Jonathan Gibson (Cambridge: D. S. Brewer, 1997), 293–313, 297.

68. Perhaps the poem addresses fourteenth-century church corruption that resulted from legalism; Hatt, *God and the Gawain Poet*, 101. Bonaventure accused the early leaders of the church, and especially Peter, of falling into the sin of legalism, which maintained the validity of the Law. And Bonaventure saw this legalism as persisting throughout church history in "attempt[s] to take something from the ecclesial convocation, such as a ministry, an office, or even a charism, as one's own by right that one claims to have earned in some way." C. Colt. Anderson, "Bonaventure and the Sin of the Church," *Theological Studies* 63 (2002): 667–89, 681–83.

69. Hatt, *God and the Gawain Poet*, 101.

70. Cohen argues that *SGGK* moralizes against "the dangers of excess, of too much faith in the physical, private, and domestic—that is, in the feminine." Cohen, *Of Giants*, 149. Caroline Walker Bynum has observed that very little evidence exists to support the notion that medieval people gendered physicality as female: "Why All the Fuss about the Body? A Medievalist's Perspective," *Critical Inquiry* 22, no. 1 (1995): 1–33, 17.

71. Gawain laments his "surfet," but the *MED* cites this usage in particular in its definition of the word as "misdeed, transgression, crime," and Gawain clarifies that he has committed an act of cowardice, covetousness, and untruth, not gluttony (ll. 2433, 2508–9). Gawain has not overindulged but has broken a vow.

And Gawain clearly does not retain the girdle's physical properties: "Bot wered not this ilk wyye for wele this gordel, / For pryde of the pendauntes, thagh polyst thay were, / And thagh the glyterande golde glent upon endes, / Bot for to saven himself when suffer hym byhoved" (ll. 2037–40). Shoaf (*The Poem as Green Girdle*, 66ff.) calls Gawain's relationship with the girdle idolatrous.

72. Also, fourteenth-century alliterative lines less often employ the traditional caesura, so that the whole verse becomes the unit of syntax, rather than the hemistitch. For an analysis of the differences between Old English alliteration and Middle English alliteration, and for a summary of the scholarship, see Martin J. Duffell, *A New History of English Metre* (London: Maney, 2008), 59–71. Note that, as an exception to the general rule, Richard Osberg views the half-verse as the primary syntactic and rhythmic unit of *Pearl*: "The Prosody of Middle English 'Pearl' and the Alliterative Lyric Tradition," in *English Historical Metrics*, ed. C. B. McCully and J. J. Anderson (New York: Cambridge University Press, 1996), 150–66, 151.

73. See Fred C. Robinson, *Beowulf and the Appositive Style* (Knoxville: University of Tennessee Press, 1985); John D. Niles, "Ring Composition and the Structure of *Beowulf*," *PMLA* 94, no. 5 (1979): 924–35.

74. Langland, *Piers*, C.VI.398–401, 410–13. Translation from *William Langland's Piers Plowman—The C Version: A Verse Translation*, trans. George Economou (Philadelphia: University of Pennsylvania Press, 1996).

75. "Instead of a well-ordered and beautifully proportioned whole," *Piers Plowman* became "a wild and luxuriant work which apparently outgrew and overgrew its original general plan," a poem whose parts dilate "with no strict relation to their importance." George Kane, *Middle English Literature: A Critical Study of the Romances, the Religious Lyrics, "Piers Plowman"* (London: Methuen, 1951), 243.

76. Miriam Edlich-Muth, *Malory and His European Contemporaries: Adapting Late Arthurian Romance Collections* (Cambridge: D. S. Brewer, 2014), 77; see also Vinaver, *Rose of Romance*, 69–72. James Parker Oakden surveys and aesthetically critiques all of the extant alliterative romances and comes to the same general conclusions about alliterative romance. Oakden calls *William of Palerne* "long-drown-out" and "wearisome," sees *The Awntyrs of Arthure* as " unconnected," and asserts that *Golarus and Gawain* suffers from "the same weakness of construction": *The Poetry of the Alliterative Revival* (Manchester: Manchester University Press, 1937), 39, 48–49. Oakden posits that *SGGK* is the only work free from "serious digressions" and not afflicted by "the customary incoherence of such works" (46).

77. Vinaver, *Rose of Romance*, 69–74.

78. Cohen, *Of Giants*, 151.

79. The *Gawain*-Poet is a kind of vernacular theologian. Nicholas Watson, "The *Gawain*-Poet as a Vernacular Theologian," 295.

80. Christine Chism, *Alliterative Revivals* (Philadelphia: University of Pennsylvania Press, 2002), 7.

4. THE FORESKIN OF MARRIAGE

1. This chapter's epigraph is from Jerome, *Select Letters*, trans. F. A. Wright (Cambridge, MA: Harvard University Press, 1933), 471.

2. Sachi Shimomura, *Odd Bodies and Visible Ends in Medieval Literature* (New York: Palgrave, 2006), 138ff.

3. W. W. Skeat, *The Complete Works of Geoffrey Chaucer*, vol. 5: *Notes to the Canterbury Tales* (Oxford: Clarendon, 1894), 295.

4. Whereas some readings might corroborate what Glenn Burger calls a "stabilizing approach to gender," I see the *praeputium*—in its doubleness and ambiguity, as emblem of the literal and/or figurative—as integral to how, as Burger puts it, "conjugality opens up a 'middle' role for women": *Chaucer's Queer Nation* (Minneapolis: University of Minnesota Press, 2002), 89.

5. The bibliography on this question is extensive but probably needs to be gathered into a future article. For now, consider that Jacques Derrida likened the excised prepuce to a wedding ring; see Thomas Docherty, *Aesthetic Democracy* (Stanford, CA: Stanford University Press, 2006), 16. Also, note that a survey of circumcision globally shows that "the only timing element common to all circumcising societies in [their] sample is that the operation always occurs before marriage." Karen Ericksen Paige and Jeffrey M. Paige, *The Politics of Reproductive Ritual* (Berkeley: University of California Press, 1981), 150; see also Charles Weiss, "Motives for Male Circumcision among Preliterate and Literate Peoples," *Journal of Sex Research* 2, no. 2 (1966): 69–88. For the connection in Islamic cultures, see S. A. Aldeeb Abu-Sahlieh, "Jehova, His Cousin Allah, and Sexual Mutilations," in *Sexual Mutilations: A Human Tragedy*, ed. George C. Denniston and Marilyn Fayre Milos (New York: Springer Science+Business Media, 1997), 41–63, 50; Edward Westermarck, *Ritual and Belief in Morocco* (New York: Routledge, 2014), 2:423; Vincent Crapanzano, *Hermes' Dilemma and Hamlet's Desire: On the Epistemology of Interpretation* (Cambridge, MA: Harvard University Press, 1992), 271; Sayyid Hamid Hurriez, *Folklore and Folklife in the United Arab Emirates* (New York: Routledge, 2002), 94; Clifford Geertz, *The Religion of Java* (Chicago: University of Chicago Press, 1960), 51; Abdelwahab Bouhdiba, *Sexuality in Islam* (New York: Routledge, 1975), 183; and Azam Torab, *Performing Islam: Gender and Ritual in Islam* (Boston: Brill, 2007), 189. For the connection in Judaism, see Theodor Gaster, *The Holy and the Profane: Evolution of Jewish Folkways* (New York: Morrow, 1980), 49; Yoram Bilu, "Circumcision, the First Haircut, and the Torah: Ritual and Male Identity among the Ultraorthodox Community of Contemporary Israel," in *Imagined Masculinities: Male Identity and Culture in the Modern Middle East*, ed. M. Ghoussoub and E. Sinclair-Webb (London: Saqi, 2000), 33–63, 37; and John T. Willis, *Yahweh and Moses in Conflict: The Role of Exodus 4:24–26 in the Book of Exodus* (New York: Peter Lang, 2010), 90. For how the connection structures Christian understandings of circumcision, see Marianne Blickenstaff, *"While the Bridegroom is with them": Marriage, Family, Gender, and Violence in the Gospel of Matthew* (London: T&T Clark, 2005), 17–19; and Tom Holland, *Romans:*

The Divine Marriage: A Biblical Theological Commentary (Eugene, OR: Pickwick, 2011), 120.

6. My translation of Jerome, "Commentarius in Epistolam S. Pauli ad Galatas," in PL 26 (Paris: Migne, 1884), 331–467, 472.

7. In *De sacramentis*, Hugh treats what he calls marriage's two forms in his chapter "De duplici institutione conjugii": Hugh of Saint Victor, *Opera omnia* (Paris: Migne, 1854), 2:481.

8. Hugh of Saint Victor, *Opera omnia*, 2:481.

9. Hugh of Saint Victor, *Opera omnia*, 2:481.

10. So, consummation does not constitute a metric for judging a marriage's validity, since true marriage might exist even without consummation. Hugh of Saint Victor, *Operà omnia*, 2:481. Furthermore, Hugh posits that even the notion of consent—so important in Hugh's promotion of conjugal marriage—must also align with spiritual priorities. Hugh argues that legitimate consent (*consensum legitimum*) exists only in those cases where both parties mutually and reciprocally consent to the constraints of marriage (2:434–35). Conjugal marriage entails not simple consent but a consent ordered toward the Augustinian goods of marriage. Hugh's theory of consent serves, then, to distinguish spiritual marriage from fleshly marriage.

11. Hugh himself had theorized the sacraments by extending Augustinian sign theory. Philip L. Reynolds, *How Marriage Became One of the Sacraments: The Sacramental Theology of Marriage from Its Medieval Origins to the Council of Trent* (Cambridge: Cambridge University Press, 2016), 421.

12. Reynolds, *How Marriage Became One of the Sacraments*, 421.

13. Reynolds, *How Marriage Became One of the Sacraments*, 421.

14. Reynolds, *How Marriage Became One of the Sacraments*, 421.

15. Reynolds, *How Marriage Became One of the Sacraments*, 422.

16. Reynolds, *How Marriage Became One of the Sacraments*, 422.

17. Reynolds, *How Marriage Became One of the Sacraments*, 443.

18. Glenn Burger (*Chaucer's Queer Nation*, 65) has pointed out that, when medieval thinkers made marriage "new," the emerging notion of marital affection "consisted of two parts, an inner reality and an outer expression."

19. Susan Joan Koslow, "The Chevrot Altarpiece: Its Sources, Meaning, and Significance," PhD diss., New York University, 1972, 37.

20. "Matrimonium a Christo commendatur, Dum sponsa sanguinum in carne copulatur. Exodi IIII capitulo." Koslow, "The Chevrot Altarpiece," 28.

21. "Conjugium tamen verum, et verum conjugii sacramentum esse, etiam si carnale commercium non fuerit subsecutum, imo potius tanto verius et sanctius esse, quanto in se nihil habet unde castitas crubescat, sed unde charitas glorietur." Koslow, "The Chevrot Altarpiece," 432. The scroll text provides cryptic advice, and Koslow puts forth a plausible but, in my view, unpersuasive reading of the text. Koslow asserts that "the implication is that only after the bride is deflorated is the marriage consummated. Since Matrimony was considered an image of Christ's

union with the Church, the Church being His bride, the text must also be considered in a figurative sense. Only after the Crucifixion when Christ's blood was shed, was He united with His spouse" (38). In general, medieval theologians and canonists did not accept that consummation validated a marriage. In fact, Hugh had argued that true marriage could exist based upon consent alone, and he asserted that marriage became more sacred precisely when it least involved intercourse.

22. For Hugh, matrimony's binding of the flesh refers to the Incarnational marriage of Christ and Ecclesia: He describes the fleshly union of the Incarnation as a type with the "office" of marriage but goes on to say that the sacrament of marriage can still take place without such fleshly unions.

23. Catherine of Siena, *The Letters of Catherine of Siena*, trans. Suzanne Noffke (Arizona Center for Medieval and Renaissance Studies, 2007), 2:184. Early modern Catholics referred to Catherine of Siena as the *sponsa sanguinum*; see Joanna Baptista Rovera, ed., *S. Catharina virgo et martyr sponsa sanguinum celebrata* (Vienna: Typis Matthaei Cosmerovii, 1668). This figure rewrites the gender of the preputial wedding band: The *sponsus sanguinum* of Exodus becomes feminine. Christ's Foreskin symbolized this mystical matrimony.

24. Geert Lernout, "Collector of Prepuces: Foreskins in *Ulysses*," *James Joyce Quarterly* 44, no. 2 (2007): 345–52, 349.

25. My reading of the Wife responds to the current scholarship. As I explain, my method is modeled after Carolyn Dinshaw's approach to Chaucer's "sexual poetics," but I differ from Dinshaw in my understanding of how patristic literary theory operates. Also, my concern for narratological issues adds a structural dimension to Burger's suggestion that the *Tales* deploy marriage as a means for rethinking medieval relations between the body and the community and in turn for negotiating a move toward modernity. Dinshaw has argued that the Wife of Bath—in both her hermeneutic approach and in her self-presentation—represents "the literal body of the text that itself has signifying value and leads to the spirit without its necessarily being devalued or destroyed in the process": Carolyn Dinshaw, *Chaucer's Sexual Poetics* (Madison: University of Wisconsin Press, 1989), 114. Scholes and Kellogg also described the Wife as an allegorical representation of carnality, while Patterson suggested that the Wife's engagement with exegesis highlights the carnality of language. Robert Scholes and Robert Kellogg, *The Nature of Narrative* (New York: Oxford University Press, 1966), 92; Lee Patterson, "'For the Wyves Love of Bathe': Feminine Rhetoric and Poetic Resolution in the *Roman de la Rose* and the *Canterbury Tales*," *Speculum* 58 (1983): 656–95, 677. Graham D. Caie calls the Wife a "fake exegete" and observes that she interprets overly literally and relies on erroneous or partial citations of Scripture and theology: "The Significance of Marginal Glosses in the Earliest Manuscripts of the *Canterbury Tales*," in *Chaucer and Scriptural Tradition*," ed. David Lyle Jeffrey (Ottawa: University of Ottawa Press, 1984), 75–88, 75. And Peggy Knapp regards the Wife as a "theorist of interpretation" who is directly influenced by Augustine's *On Christian Doctrine*: "Wandrynge by the weye: On Alisoun and Augustine," in *Medieval Texts*

and Contemporary Readers, ed. Laurie A. Finke and Martin B. Shichtman (Ithaca, NY: Cornell University Press, 1987), 142–57, 142. For me, these insights allow for a reading of the Wife that, while aware of her engagement with patristic theory, does not indignantly moralize in the Robertsonian manner; see S. H. Rigby, *Chaucer in Context: Society, Allegory, and Gender* (Manchester: Manchester University Press, 1996), 77. Robertson regarded all medieval literature allegorically, reading Chaucer in terms of a quest for Christian truth; Steve Ellis, "Introduction," in *Chaucer: The Canterbury Tales*, ed. Steve Ellis (New York: Taylor & Francis, 1999), 1–22, 3. But Delany has suggested that Chaucer's "pluralistic impulse" challenges the medieval exegetical tradition (see Ellis, "Introduction," 3). And, in this vein, Dinshaw's work proposes that, while Chaucer may have engaged patristic literary theory, he did not necessarily intend thereby to advocate for it. Moreover, Charles A. Owen Jr. has proposed that the *Tales* take an interest in morality mostly as a comic motif: "Morality as a Comic Motif in the *Canterbury Tales*," *College English* 16 (1955): 226–32. And, as Philip West has argued, the Wife engages with Pauline theories of textuality primarily for the sake of parody: "The Perils of Pauline Theology: The *Wife of Bath's Prologue* and *Tale*," *Essays in Arts and Sciences* 8 (1979): 7–16, 16. I see the Wife's engagement with patristic theory as highly ironic.

As I have already made clear, I differ somewhat from Dinshaw in my understanding of how patristic hermeneutics uses the body to think about textuality. According to Dinshaw (*Chaucer's Sexual Poetics*, 113–14), patristic literary theory constructs the literal as feminine: "Woman is associated with the body and the text—as in the Pauline exegetical assimilation of literality and carnality to femininity . . . and is opposed to the gloss, written by men." Patterson argues that the Wife's association of textuality with her body reflects a medieval view that poetic language is sexual and feminine. And so, in *The Canterbury Tales*, Dinshaw proposes that "out of this company of 'goode men' the voice of the woman bursts: 'Nay, by my fader soule, that schal he nat! . . . He schal no gospel glosen here ne teche.' Instead, 'My joly body schal a tale telle,' a tale having nothing to do with 'philosophie, / Ne phislyas, ne termes queinte of law.' The Wife opposes her tale to the 'lerned men's' lore: it is her 'joly body' against their oppressive teaching and glossing." Dinshaw, *Chaucer's Sexual Poetics*, 113. But this reading depends upon a textual emendation by E. Talbot Donaldson, who attributes the lines to the Wife. Robert Pratt argues in support of Donaldson's reading: "The Development of the Wife of Bath," in *Studies in Medieval Literature in Honor of Professor Albert Croll Baugh*, ed. MacEdward Leach (Philadelphia: University of Pennsylvania Press, 1961), 45–49. But all extant manuscripts attribute these lines to male figures, either to the Shipman, Summoner, or Squire; see Larry D. Benson, ed., *The Riverside Chaucer* (New York: Oxford University Press, 2008), 1126. The textual evidence suggests, then, that Chaucer's medieval readers did not subscribe strictly to the view that feminine textual bodies always oppose masculine glossing. Furthermore, Katherine Heinrichs has argued that patristic thinkers did not associate all women with carnality, but in certain respects they actually developed an egalitarian gender politics: "Tropological Woman in Chaucer: Literary Elaborations of an Exegetical Tradition," *English Studies* 76 (1995): 209–14, 213; see also Leo Carruthers, "*No woman of no clerk is preysed*: Attitudes to Women in Medieval English Religious Literature," in *A Wyf Ther Was: Essays in Honor of Paule Mertens-Fonck*, ed. Juliette Dor. Liège (Université de Liège, 1992), 49–60, 60. Chaucer's medieval readers imagined that the "joly body" of a man might also oppose the learned gloss just as well as any female body.

26. Graham D. Caie, "The Significance of Marginal Glosses in the Earliest Manuscripts of the *Canterbury Tales*," in *Chaucer and Scriptural Tradition*, ed. David Lyle Jeffrey (Ottawa: University of Ottawa Press, 1984), 75–88, 77.

27. Susan Schibanoff, "The New Reader and Female Textuality in Two Early Commentaries on Chaucer," *Studies in the Age of Chaucer* 10 (1988): 71–108, 107.

28. Skeat, *Complete Works of Geoffrey Chaucer*, V.295.

29. All citations of *The Canterbury Tales* are from Benson, ed., *The Riverside Chaucer*, by line number (fragment III, group D). Translation from *The Canterbury Tales*, trans. David Wright (New York: Oxford University Press 1985), by page number. Note that my review of the scholarship on the Wife of Bath has relied on Peter G. Beidler and Elizabeth M. Biebel, *Chaucer's Wife of Bath's Prologue and Tale: An Annotated Bibliography, 1900 to 1995* (Toronto: University of Toronto Press, 1998).

30. "Qui uxorem habet, et debitor dicitur, et esse in praeputio, et servus uxoris." Skeat, *Complete Works*, V.295.

31. See Alcuin Blamires, "Love, Marriage, Sex, Gender," in *Chaucer and Religion*, ed. Helen Phillips (Cambridge: D. S. Brewer, 2010), 3–23, 18.

32. Lawrence Besserman, "*Glosynge is a glorious thyng*: Chaucer's Biblical Exegesis," in *Chaucer and Scriptural Tradition*, ed. David Lyle Jeffrey (Ottawa: University of Ottawa Press, 1984), 65–73, 66; Douglas Wurtele, "Chaucer's *Canterbury Tales* and Nicholas of Lyre's *Postillae literalis et moralis super totam Bibliam*," in *Chaucer and Scriptural Tradition*, ed. David Lyle Jeffrey (Ottawa: University of Ottawa Press, 1984), 89–107, 104.

33. The Pardoner's stated wish to remain circumcised of women provides a pretense for hiding his desire to "drynken of another tonne" (or "cask"; l. 170).

34. Glenn Burger argued that the Pardoner's queerness destabilizes medieval gender categories and, later, that the kiss between the Host and the Pardoner entails embracing masculinity's deconstruction: "Queer Chaucer," *English Studies in Canada* 20 (1994): 153–70, 162–63; "Kissing the Pardoner," *Publications of the Modern Language Association* 107 (1992): 1143–56, 1152. Steven F. Kruger argued for seeing the Pardoner as a gay figure who disrupts heterosexual constructs: "Claiming the Pardoner: Toward a Gay Reading of Chaucer's Pardoner's Tale," *Exemplaria* 6, no. 1 (1994): 115–39, 137. Dinshaw suggested that the Pardoner reveals the inadequacy of male/female spirit/letter binaries, that his body proposes a letter devoid of spirit, and later that he marks the incompleteness of heterosexuality. Carolyn Dinshaw, *Chaucer's Sexual Poetics*, 157; Carolyn Dinshaw, "Chaucer's

Queer Touches/A Queer Touches Chaucer," *Exemplaria* 7, no. 1 (1995): 92. For a review of the scholarship on the Pardoner's sexuality, see Marilyn Sutton, *Chaucer's Pardoner's Prologue and Tale: An Annotated Bibliography, 1900 to 1995* (Toronto: Toronto University Press, 2000), esp. xlix–li.

35. R. M. Lumiansky, *Of Sondry Folk: The Dramatic Principle in the Canterbury Tales* (Austin: University of Texas Press, 1955), 8.

36. Anne Kernan, "The Archwife and the Eunuch," *English Literary History* 41 (1974): 1–25, 25.

37. See Sherman Hawkins, "Chaucer's Prioress and the Sacrifice of Praise," *Journal of English and Germanic Philology* 63, no. 4 (1964): 599–624, 623.

38. As Hawkins ("Chaucer's Prioress," 623) writes, "the Pardoner reduces Christianity to a code as rigorous and external as the old law itself: He is inwardly a Jew of the kind described in [Romans 2] verses 17–24."

39. On Freud's conflation of circumcision and castration, see Jay Geller, *On Freud's Jewish Body: Mitigating Circumcisions* (New York: Fordham University Press, 2007), 25.

40. Rita Copeland, "The Pardoner's Body and the Disciplining of Rhetoric," in *Framing Medieval Bodies*, ed. Sarah Kay and Miri Rubin (Manchester: Manchester University Press, 1994), 138–59, 149.

41. See Jennifer Smith, "Shaving, Circumcision, Blood, and Sin: Gendering the Audience in John Mirk's Sermons," in *Venus & Mars: Engendering Love and War in Medieval and Early Modern Europe*, ed. Andrew Lynch and Philippa Maddern (Nedlands: University of Western Australia Press, 1995), 106–18, 113.

42. David A. Jeffrey, *A Dictionary of Biblical Tradition in English Literature* (Grand Rapids, MI: Eerdmans, 1992), 219.

43. Kara Virginia Donaldson, "Alisoun's Language: Body, Text, and Glossing in Chaucer's *The Miller's Tale*," *Philological Quarterly* 71 (1992): 139–53, 142.

44. Karma Lochrie, *Heterosyncracies: Female Sexuality When Normal Wasn't* (Minneapolis: University of Minnesota Press, 2005), 95. Lochrie writes, "the 1425 Middle English edition of the *Cyrurgie of Guy de Chauliac* describes as part of the female sexual anatomy the 'priue schappe or chose' that he analogizes to the foreskin of the penis. John Trevisa's 1398 translation of Bartholomwe Anglicus's *De Proprietatibus Rerum* also identifies the female 'privy chose' by way of comparison with the male 'yerd' and the anatomy of the female ape. The Wife of Bath's *bele chose* is one of the only Middle English literary uses of the term *chose* to mean 'private part,' but more importantly, it may be one of the rare instances where female sexual pleasure is so directly (and anatomically) invoked)" (95). Galen also saw the pudendum as the mirror image of the *praeputium*; see Robert Darby, *A Surgical Temptation: The Demonization of the Foreskin and the Rise of Circumcision in Britain* (Chicago: University of Chicago Press, 2005), 119.

45. "Was the Wife of Bath Jewish?" Leslie Fielder asked; see Paul Szarmach, *Aspects of Jewish Culture in the Middle Ages: An Overview and Synthesis* (Albany: SUNY Press, 1979), 205.

46. As discussed in Geller, *Freud's Jewish Body*, 8–9.

47. D. W. Robertson makes this comparison in a footnote: *A Preface to Chaucer: Studies in Medieval Perspectives* (Princeton, NJ: Princeton University Press, 1962), 331n96. And Sara Lipton points to the Wife's description of bad wifely behavior in her analysis of Synagoga, explaining that "because Holy Church is traditionally construed in Christian exegesis as the bride of Christ, and therefore exemplifies specifically wifely as well as generally Christian virtues, her counterpart—Synagoga—would logically take on all the characteristics of a bad wife": "The Temple Is My Body: Gender, Carnality, and Synagoga in the *Bible Moralisée*," in *Imagining the Self, Imagining the Other: Visual Representation and Jewish-Christian Dynamics in the Middle Ages and Early Modern Period*, ed. Eva Frojmovic (Leiden: Brill, 2002), 129–64, 140. Lipton cites the Wife as a prime example of such bad, synagogue-esque wives. Likewise, S. H. Rigby (*Chaucer in Context*, 159) points out that contemporary conduct manuals describe good and bad wives in terms of Ecclesia and Synagoga. Additionally, Megan McLaughlin has observed that Honorius Augustodunensis, in a dialogue between Ecclesia and Synagoga about whom they could marry, depicted the former as an allegorizer and the latter as a literalist: *Sex, Gender, and Episcopal Authority in an Age of Reform, 1000–1122* (Cambridge: Cambridge University Press, 2010), 229. More generally, Christine M. Rose also has observed correspondences between Synagoga and other female figures in Chaucer: "The Jewish Mother-in-Law: Synagoga and the *Man of Law's Tale*," on *Chaucer and the Jews: Sources, Contexts, Meanings*, ed. Sheila Delany (New York: Routledge, 2002), 3–24.

48. Edmund Reiss, "Biblical Parody: Chaucer's 'Distortions' of Scripture," in *Chaucer and Scriptural Tradition*, ed. David Lyle Jeffrey (Ottawa: University of Ottawa Press, 1984), 47–61.

49. Robertson, *A Preface to Chaucer*, 326.

50. If, in patriarchal discourse, where women have no claim to the text, then "she is *the* text." Thomas Hanh, "Teaching the Resistant Woman: The Wife of Bath and the Academy," *Exemplaria* 4 (1992): 431–40, 438.

51. Of course, the Wife also resembles other types. Dean D. Fansler argues that the Wife is an adaptation of the figure of La Vieille from *Roman de la Rose*, in *Chaucer and the Roman de la Rose* (New York: Columbia University Press, 1914), 168; on the differences between the Wife and La Vieille, see also Patricia Margaret Kean, *The Art of Narrative: Chaucer and the Making of English Poetry* (London: Routledge, 1972), 2:154. But perhaps the Wife is so intriguing because she resists type. Derek Pearsall believes that, by giving the Wife a contemporary location and social status, Chaucer translates the Wife out of an iconographic tradition: *The Canterbury Tales* (London: George Allen and Unwin, 1985), 81. Burger questions the persistence of seeing the Wife as a real person (*Chaucer's Queer Nation*, 82), and Susan Crane has argued against the many attempts to read the Wife psychologically in "Alison of Bath Accused of Murder: Case Dismissed," *English Language Notes* 25 (1988): 10–15, 15. R. W. Hanning recognizes that the Wife has herself been

glossed as an antifeminist stereotype: "'I shall finde it in a maner glose': Versions of Textual Harassment in Medieval Literature," in *Medieval Texts and Contemporary Readers*, ed. Laurie A. Finke and Martin B. Shichtman (Ithaca, NY: Cornell University Press, 1987), 27–50, 50. Roger Ellis notes that the Prologue is a compilation of reported or direct speech in "Persona and Voice: Plain Speaking in Three Canterbury Tales," *Bulletin of the John Rylands University Library* 74 (1992): 121–39, 131. George Kane points out that the Prologue's excessive details make the Wife seem more lifelike: *Chaucer* (Oxford: Oxford University Press, 1984), 98. I suspect that the attempt to read her as a person—rather than as a gloss—follows from a kind of pre-Pauline refusal to fully allegorize and to come to terms with the completely radical proposition that there is neither "male nor female."

52. Arthur K. Moore, "Alysoun's Other Tonne," *Modern Language Notes* 59 (1944): 481–83, 481.

53. The Wife's Prologue follows Vinsauf's guidelines for amplification. Edgar H. Duncan, "Chaucer's 'Wife of Bath's Prologue,' Lines 193–828, and Geoffrey of Vinsauf's *Documentum*," *Modern Philology* 66 (1969): 199–211, 199.

54. Edward Wagenknecht, *The Personality of Chaucer* (Norman: University of Oklahoma Press, 1968), 95.

55. Warren S. Smith suggests that the Wife here adopts an Augustinian position on marriage: "The Wife of Bath Debates Jerome," *Chaucer Review* 32, no. 2 (1997): 129–45, 129.

56. Smith, "The Wife of Bath Debates Jerome," 135.

57. John Mahoney, "Alice of Bath: Her 'secte' and 'gentil text,'" *Criticism* 6 (1964): 144–55, 146. And see, again, Smith, "The Wife of Bath Debates Jerome," 135.

58. As Bernard Felix Huppé points out, the Wife invokes the Augustinian understanding of the text—but only in order to ignore Augustine, "in favor of her own gloss, which reads into the text an encouragement to be active in her favorite amusement": *A Reading of the Canterbury Tales* (Albany: SUNY Press, 1964), 111.

59. On the hermeneutic spectrum, the Wife's position has more in common with Augustine's plain allegory than with Jerome's numerology, but the Wife is plainer still than Augustine.

60. See *Middle English Dictionary*, s.v. "ğentĭl" (Ann Arbor: Regents of the University of Michigan, 2018), https://quod.lib.umich.edu/m/middle-english-dictionary/dictionary/MED18402. Burger sees the term "gentil" as elastic, undecidable, and unstable (*Chaucer's Queer Nation*, 53–59). And A. C. Spearing argues that the gentle/Gentile pun informs *The Franklin's Tale*, whose pagan characters explore how "gentilesse" does not result from genealogy: *Medieval to Renaissance in English Poetry* (Cambridge: Cambridge University Press, 1985).

61. See Spearing, *Medieval to Renaissance*, 40–41. As Spearing points out, *Piers Plowman* describes this supersessionary theology in terms of "gentil men": Langland notes that "The Jewes, that were gentil men, Jesu thei despised" so that Christians became "gentil men with Jesu" (B.XIX. 35, 40; qtd. in Spearing, *Medieval to Renaissance*, 42–43).

62. For example, when John Trevisa explicates this passage: "In þe membres genytal god haþ send suche an appetite inseperable þat eueriche beest schulde be comfortid to multeplie beestis of his owne kynde"; 60b/a.

63. Hanning ("I Shall," 19–20) notes this pun as well.

64. The Wife's views on glossing change: She views glossing as misogynistic, later as pleasurable; Winthrop Wetherbee, *Geoffrey Chaucer: The Canterbury Tales* (Cambridge: Cambridge University Press, 1989), 84. I mean to point out that, in both cases, she sees it as erotic. Likewise, Rodney Delasanta argues that *quoniam* has ecclesiastical connotations, so that this sex pun equates the vagina with something divine: "*Quoniam* and the Wife of Bath," *PLL* 8 (1972): 202–6, 202.

65. The Wife's reading of Gen. 1:28 does not conform to the kind of allegorical process by which Augustine sees the text as an injunction to Christian marriage, but the Wife describes her reading as gentil/Gentile.

66. Curiously, Stewart Justman points out that, by noting inconsistencies in Paul's epistles, the Wife actually resembles Jerome: "Medieval Monism and Abuse of Authority in Chaucer," *Chaucer Review* 11 (1976): 95–111, 102.

67. As Dinshaw (*Chaucer's Sexual Poetics*, 120) writes, the Wife's Prologue and *Tale* create an "allegorical representation of the act of reading."

68. Seth Lerer, "*The Canterbury Tales*," in *The Yale Companion to Chaucer*, ed. Seth Lerer (New Haven, CT: Yale University Press, 2006), 243–94, 258.

69. Laurie Finke, "'All is for to selle': Breeding Capital in the *Wife of Bath's Prologue and Tale*," in *The Wife of Bath*, ed. Peter G. Beidler (Boston: St. Martin's, 1996), 171–88, 171.

70. As Paul E. Beichner points out, Jankyn's story of a man with three wives—while ostensibly an allegorical fable—seems designed to aggravate the Wife and therefore is not properly allegorical: "The Allegorical Interpretation of Medieval Literature," *Publications of the Modern Language Association* 82 (1967): 33–38, 38.

71. H. Marshall Leicester Jr., "'My bed was ful of verray blood': Subject, Dream, and Rape in the *Wife of Bath's Prologue and Tale*," in *The Wife of Bath*, ed. Peter G. Beidler (Boston: St. Martin's, 1996), 234–54, 234.

72. Peter Brown and Andrew Butcher describe the world of fairy as an "alternative authority" in *The Age of Saturn: Literature and History in the Canterbury Tales* (Oxford: Basil Blackwell, 1991), 37.

73. See ll. 1000, 1004, 1063, 1072, 1100, 1110, 1118, 1131, 1154, 1160, 1172, 1207, 1215, 1210, 1213.

74. Alfred David, "Old, New, and Yong in Chaucer," *Studies in the Age of Chaucer* 15 (1993): 5–21, 16.

75. Russell A. Peck, "Biblical Interpretation: St. Paul and the *Canterbury Tales*," in *Chaucer and Scriptural Tradition*, ed. David Lyle Jeffrey (Ottawa: University of Ottawa Press, 1984), 143–70, 158.

76. This is the tale's "moral climax," according to Douglas Gray, "Chaucer and Gentilesse," in *One Hundred Years of English Studies in Dutch Universities:*

Seventeen Papers Read at the Centenary Conference, Groningen, 15–16 Jan. 1986, ed. G. H. V. Bunt et al. (Amsterdam: Rodopi, 1987), 1–27, 18.

77. See Skeat, *The Complete Works of Geoffrey Chaucer*, I.552–54, V.319. The Chaucerian gentilesse is an admixture of religious and social perspectives, according to Helen Phillips, "Morality in the *Canterbury Tales*, Chaucer's Lyrics, and the *Legend of Good Women*," in *Chaucer and Religion*, ed. Helen Phillips (Cambridge: D. S. Brewer, 2010), 156–74, 171.But Nevill Coghill argues that Chaucer views gentilesse as specifically Christian: *Chaucer's Idea of What Is Noble* (Oxford: Oxford University Press, 1971), 15; and Gloria K. Shapiro argues that the Wife's "sermon" on gentilesse reveals the basically religious nature of her character: "Dame Alice as Deceptive Narrator," *Chaucer Review* 6 (1971): 130–41, 131.

78. See ll. 1109, 1111, 1115, 1116, 1117, 1130, 1134, 1137, 1146, 1152, 1153, 1156, 1157, 1159, 1162, twice in 1170, 1175, 1209, 1211.

79. "When the foul old wife, the heroine of the *Tale*, transforms herself into her fair young incarnation, her change abruptly truncates her narrative." Shimomura, *Odd Bodies*, 138.

80. Burger, *Chaucer's Queer Nation*, 48.

81. See Burger, *Chaucer's Queer Nation*, 78. As Burger argues, the Wife's insistence upon personal experience "suggests an engagement with the present that is significantly different from the masculinist clerical hermeneutic she argues with" (80). Moreover, "Rather than simply pointing 'back' to a transcendent, originary moment in the past or 'outside' to the frame of some hegemonic authority, the Wife claims to occupy a present that is its own moment" (80).

82. As David Williams suggests, the Wife escapes from the present by insisting upon an experience that consists of sex and power; she desires the past and anticipates the future: *The Canterbury Tales: A Literary Pilgrimage* (Boston: Twayne, 1987), 66.

83. What Burger (*Chaucer's Queer Nation*, x) calls the "anxieties that such a departure from the past provokes."

84. David Aers points out that, however much the Wife protests Pauline theology, she remains trapped within its systems: *Chaucer, Langland, and the Creative Imagination* (London: Routledge, 1980), 149. On the other hand, Barrie Ruth Straus argues that, even though the Wife becomes enclosed in masculine discourse, she undermines this discourse: "The Subversive Discourse of the Wife of Bath: Phallocentric Discourse and the Imprisonment of Criticism," *English Literary History* 55 (1988): 527–54, 528. Yet a third possibility: Catherine Cox points out that the Wife's poetics is ambivalent and provides no clear solutions to the interrelationships between gender and language: "Holy Erotica and the Virgin Word: Promiscuous Glossing in the *Wife of Bath's Prologue*," *Exemplaria* 5 (1993): 207–37, 237. And Minnis offers that, though "fallible," the Wife nevertheless provides useful instruction: *Fallible Authors: Chaucer's Pardoner and Wife of Bath* (Philadelphia: University of Pennsylvania Press, 2007), 245.

85. Joseph J. Mogan Jr., "Chaucer and the *Bona Matrimonii*," *Chaucer Review* 4 (1970): 123–41, 123. And/or the Wife views woman's sovereignty and the divine origin of gentilesse as equivalent, according to Donald C. Baker, "Chaucer's Clerk and the Wife of Bath on the Subject of *Gentilesse*," *Studies in Philology* 59 (1962): 631–40, 634. Similarly, James W. Cook argues that Wife's goal of sexual gratification means that her marriages cannot attain sacramental grace: "'That she was out of alle charitee': Point-Counterpoint in the *Wife of Bath's Prologue* and *Tale*," *Chaucer Review* 13 (1978): 51–65, 52. Sister Mary Raynelda Makarewicz points out that the Wife's desire for sovereignty is a species of the pride that also leads her to lechery: *The Patristic Influence on Chaucer* (Washington, DC: Catholic University of America Press, 1953), 191. And the Hag, in her argument with the Knight, appeals to the knight's sexual appetite: Robert S. Haller, "The Wife of Bath and the Three Estates," *Annuale Mediaevale* 6 (1965): 47–64, 55. Florence H. Ridley suggests that the *Pardoner's Tale* and the *Wife's Tale* are related in structure: "The Friar and the Critics," in *The Idea of Medieval Literature: New Essays on Chaucer and Medieval Culture in Honor of Donald R. Howard*, ed. James M. Dean and Christian Zacher (Newark: University of Delaware Press, 1992), 160–72, 165.

86. Paul C. Ruggiero, *The Art of the Canterbury Tales* (Madison: University of Wisconsin Press, 1965), 198. The Wife's lack of charity distinguishes her from the Lady, who saves her husband's soul: Cook, "'That she was out of alle charitee,'" *Chaucer Review* 13 (1978): 51–65, 65. The romance risks sentimentalizing the Wife: Rosemary Woolf, "Moral Chaucer and Kindly Gower," in *J. R. R. Tolkien, Scholar and Storyteller: Essays in Memoriam*, ed. Mary Salu and Robert T. Farrell (Ithaca, NY: Cornell University Press, 1979), 245. Derek Brewer likewise notes the differences between the Wife's personality and the delicate nature of the tale in *Chaucer*, 3rd ed. (London: Longman, 1973), 108.

87. See also Rose A. Zimbardo, "Unity and Duality in the *Wife of Bath's Prologue and Tale*," *Tennessee Studies in Literature* 11 (1966): 11–18, 11. Similarly, Peggy Knapp argues that the Wife's performance of the antifeminist tradition and of romance makes her both a new and a traditional female in "Alisoun of Bathe and the Reappropriation of Tradition," *Chaucer Review* 24 (1989): 45–52, 51.

88. Also, the Wife's circumcising tale puts into play a larger discussion about gentilesse, a major theme throughout the Marriage Group; see W. P. Albrecht, "The Sermon on Gentilesse," *College English* 12 (1951): 459.

CODA

1. The myth of Bumby's circumcision is told by John Leland, *A Guide to Hemingway's Paris* (New York: Algonquin, 1989), 36; Paul Mariani, *William Carlos Williams: A New World Naked* (New York: Norton, 1981), 239; James R. Mellow, *Hemingway: A Life without Consequences* (New York: Houghton Mifflin, 1992), 258; Jeffrey Meyers, *Hemingway: A Biography* (New York: Harper & Row, 1985), 125; Michael S. Reynolds, *Hemingway: The Paris Years* (New York: Blackwell, 1989), 209; Sanford J. Smoller, *Adrift among Geniuses: Robert McAlmon, Writer and Pub-*

lisher of the Twenties (Philadelphia: Pennsylvania State University Press, 1974), 137; Jack Coulehan, "William Carlos Williams Circumcises Ernest Hemingway's First Son," *Canadian Medical Association Journal* 182, no. 7 (2010): 703.

2. Williams himself explains that he retracted Bumby's foreskin; see William Carlos Williams, *The Correspondence of William Carlos Williams and Louis Zukofsky*, ed. Barry Ahearn (Middletown, CT: Wesleyan University Press, 2003), 294; Kenneth Schuyler Lynn, *Hemingway* (Cambridge, MA: Harvard University Press, 1995), 249. For one of Williams's complaints about public performances, see Paul Mariani, *William Carlos Williams: A New World Naked* (New York: Norton, 1981), 589; and Peter Middleton, "The Contemporary Poetry Reading," in *Close Listening: Poetry and the Performed Word*, ed. Charles Bernstein (New York: Oxford University Press, 1998), 262–99, 278. Note that, as a physician, Williams performed the operation so regularly that, as he related in a letter to Louis Zukofsky, circumcision cut into his poetic practice: "I do nothing but punch the typewriter these days—that is when I'm not delivering the usual quota of week-end babies (I don't mean that they're all girls)—tho' it saves money to have girls nowadays—they don't have to be circumcised" (150). Williams's life as a poet—especially his time with the typewriter—was cut up into segments, divided by week ("weak").

3. For Defoe's engagement with circumcision, see Daniel Defoe, *A Second Volume of the Writings of the Author of The True-born Englishman* (s.n., 1705), 45; and Gesine Palmer, "An Apology for Mr. Toland in a Letter to Himself," in *Religious Apologetics: Philosophical Argumentation*, ed. Yossef Schwartz and Volkhard Krech (Mohr Siebeck, 2004), 69–87, 73. For Swift, see Jonathan Swift, *The Works of Rev. Dr. Jonathan Swift* (C. Bathurst et al., 1784), 17:361–67. Note also the circumcision scene in *Tristram Shandy*, as discussed in Robert Darby, "'An Oblique and Slovenly Initiation': The Circumcision Episode in *Tristram Shandy*," *Eighteenth-Century Life* 27, no. 1 (2003): 72–84. For Emerson's brief allusion to circumcision, see "The Poet," in *Essays and Poems* (New York: Library of America, 1996), 445–68. On the foreskin in *Moby-Dick*, see Elisa New, "Bible Leaves! Bible Leaves! Hellenism and Hebraism in Melville's *Moby-Dick*," *Poetics Today* 19, no. 2 (1998): 281–303. On the foreskin in George Eliot, see K. M. Newton, *Modernizing George Eliot: The Writer as Artist, Intellectual, Proto-Modernist, Cultural Critic* (New York: Bloomsbury, 2011), esp. chap. 8.

4. In 1603, Henoch Clapham wrote that "Henrie the eight" was "like a sacramentall eight-day," who "did cut off the fore-skin of our Corruption"; see *Three Partes of Salomon his Song of Songs* (London: Valentine Sims, 1603), available at EEBO: TCP, http://quod.lib.umich.edu/e/eebo/A15991.0001.001.

5. In 1561, Inquisitors claimed Queen Elizabeth I "maintained circumcision and the Jewish laws"; see "Elizabeth: August 1561, 16–20," *Calendar of State Papers Foreign, Elizabeth*, vol. 4: *1561–1562*, ed. Joseph Stevenson (London: Her Majesty's Stationery Office, 1866), 250–66, available at British History Online, http://www.british-history.ac.uk/cal-state-papers/foreign/vol4/pp250-266.

6. See Garrett P. J. Epp, "John Foxe and the Circumcised Stage," *Exemplaria* 9,

no. 2 (1997): 281–313, 281. I might also add a few other primary sources: In 1582 Stephen Gosson attacked actors whom he called "uncircumcised Philistines"; see *Playes Confuted in Five Actions* (London: Thomas Gosson, [1582]), n.p., available at EEBO: TCP, http://quod.lib.umich.edu/e/eebo/A01951. Likewise in 1583 Phillip Stubbes expressed disdain for the "carnall man with uncircumcised heart"; see *The Anatomie of Abuses* (London: [John Kingston], 1583), n.p., available at EEBO: TCP, http://quod.lib.umich.edu/e/eebo/A13086. In 1633, William Prynne preached that a "circumcised ear" must abhor the theater and that the pious must "circumcise from thee all this demeanour of the Stage and Players"; see *Histrio-mastix: The Players Scourge* (London: E[dward] Allde, Augustine Mathewes, Thomas Cotes and W[illiam] I[ones], 1633), 219, 544–45, available at EEBO: TCP, http://name .umdl.umich.edu/A10187.0001.001.

7. On circumcision in Shakespeare, see James Shapiro, *Shakespeare and the Jews* (New York: Columbia University Press, 1996), esp. chap. 4; Daniel Boyarin, "Othello's Penis: Or, Islam in the Closet," in *Shakesqueer: A Queer Companion to the Complete Works of Shakespeare*, ed. Madhavi Menon (Durham, NC: Duke University Press, 2011), 254–62; Julia Reinhard Lupton, "Othello Circumcised: Shakespeare and the Pauline Discourse of Nations," *Representations* 57 (1997): 73–89; and Amy Greenstadt, "The Kindest Cut: Circumcision and Queer Kinship in *The Merchant of Venice*," *English Literary History* 80, no. 4 (2013): 945–80.

8. Abraham Cowley championed the Restoration of Charles II in a poem that likened the decapitation of Charles I to "the Circumcision of the chosen Race": *Poems: Miscellanies, The Mistress, Pindarique Odes, Davideis, Verses Written on Several Occasions*, ed. A. R. Waller (Cambridge: Cambridge University Press, 1905), 193. Similarly, John Gauden in 1659 claimed that "both Church and State" were "sore and circumcised" because of the war: *Ecclesiae anglicanae suspiria: The tears, sighs, complaints and prayers of the Church of England* (London: s.n., 1659), 5. Marchamont Nedham, polemicizing that Presbyterians would cause another civil war in 1677, charged that the Presbyters wanted to "circumcise the Crown": *A second pacquet of advices and animadversions* (London: Jonathan Edwin, 1677), 4. And again in 1679 an anonymous poem depicted the Civil War as an attempt to "circumcise" the monarchy: *Spectrum anti-monarchicum, or, The Ghost of Hugh Peters* (London: s.n., 1679), 2.

9. Robert Darby, *A Surgical Temptation: The Demonization of the Foreskin and the Rise of Circumcision in Britain* (Chicago: University of Chicago Press, 2005), 10.

10. Mason Locke Weems, *The Life of George Washington* (Matthew Carey, 1809), 135–36.

11. The first-century Roman agriculturalist Columella referred to skinned trunk as the "circumcisae parti": see Columella, *De arboribus*, ed. E. S. Forster and Edward H. Heffner (Cambridge, MA: Harvard University Press, 1955), 402; Catullus and Ausonius used similar figures; see J. N. Adams, *The Latin Sexual Vocabulary* (Baltimore, MD: Johns Hopkins University Press, 1982), 74. Thomas Jefferson is

known to have read Columella; see *Thomas Jefferson's Library: A Catalog with the Entries in His Own Order*, ed. James Gilreath and Douglas L. Wilson (Clark, NJ: Lawbook Exchange, 2008), 36.

12. Weems, *The Life of George Washington*, 135–36.

13. The cherry tree's circumcision fits a larger pattern of religious symbolism that Weems used throughout his biography. Indeed, the cherry-tree incident follows another, less famous anecdote in which little George refuses to share an apple with his siblings. George's father teaches the greedy boy a lesson by showing him a vast, blooming orchard. Washington—like the Adam of Genesis, newly ashamed for his theft of the fruit—hangs his head and scratches the ground "with his little naked toes." He begs his father for forgiveness. The Eden-like orchard evokes the theft from the Tree of the Knowledge of Good and Evil, and it alludes to Adam's nudity and dust-to-dust mortality.

14. Grant Wood gave eloquent visual expression to the contradictory layers of the tale in his classic painting of 1939 *Parson Weems' Fable*. In the foreground Weems, in powdered wig, attracts our focus with his forthright gaze. His left hand gestures for us to look upon the scene as Washington Sr. holds the cherry sapling, which leans back in his hand like a tango dancer. A slice of the tree's bark juts priapically from the trunk's midsection. The tree becomes anthropomorphized into an ithyphallic monument—a "body," as Weems said, shown with a penis of cut bark. Magical-realist cherries summon up drops of circumcision blood. A Gestalt image, the sapling's globular canopy also resembles a set of testicles, and the tree's trunk arcs like a dangling penis with its tip clipped off. Junior points to his hatchet. The future president, a tiny doll, wears the face of Gilbert Stuart's mythic 1797 Athenaeum portrait. In the distance two slaves pluck fruit, and storm clouds gather, reminders of what we now call, in an unfortunate metaphor, America's Original Sin. So far, Weems's posture has distracted us from his right hand. In the shadows and behind his own back, Weems pulls aside a large red curtain that frames the scene. The hand twists unnaturally, as though it does not belong to Weems. The invisible hand of this mythmaker organizes the world around the fiction of circumcised honesty.

15. See Jeremy Singer-Vine, "Snip," *Slate*, May 19, 2011, http://iscroll.dev.slate.com/articles/news_and_politics/explainer/2011/05/snip.html; and "Where Human Rights Collide: Circumcision Debate Has Berlin Searching for Answers," *Spiegel Online*, July 25, 2012, http://www.spiegel.de/international/germany/circumcision-debate-has-german-government-scrambling-for-a-law-a-846144.html; Cnaan Liphshiz, "Proposal to Ban Male Circumcision Scrapped from Finland Bill," *Times of Israel*, November 11, 2020, https://www.timesofisrael.com/proposal-to-ban-male-circumcision-scrapped-from-finland-bill/.

16. See Darby, *A Surgical Temptation*, which establishes how modern, secular circumcision derives from a Puritanical campaign to inhibit masturbation. My own thesis may be implying that there are also metaphysical underpinnings to secularity and to its covenantal sign, secular circumcision.

17. These activists produce despicable cultural products—memes and comics—that attack women and Jews, as discussed in Jeffrey Goldberg, "Foreskin Man, the Antisemitic Superhero," *Atlantic*, June 6, 2011, https://www.theatlantic.com/national/archive/2011/06/foreskin-man-the-antisemitic-superhero/239952/. But even in more mainstream venues, there is a kind of vicious racism implicit in news reports that dwell, almost pornographically, on circumcision as practiced by Jews and Muslims. The *Guardian*, for example, has published many salacious articles (with shocking photos) attacking Islamic circumcision, and the *New York Post* frequently makes hay with "Mohel Spreads Herpes" headlines.

18. See Joshua Paul Dale, "Intact or Cut? Castration and the Phallus in the New Gender Politics," *Japanese Journal of American Studies* 17 (2006): 223–44.

19. See George Lakoff and Mark Johnson, *Metaphors We Live By* (Chicago: University of Chicago Press, 1980).

20. See Jordan Osserman, "Is the Phallus Uncut? On the Role of Anatomy in Lacanian Subjectivization," *Transgender Studies Quarterly* 4, nos. 3/4 (2017): 497–517.

INDEX

The term *foreskin* is used throughout the index to denote references to *foreskin*, *praeputium* and *prepuce*. Abbreviations: *BLF* Boy with the Long Foreskin (Augustine); *PS* Peter and the Sheet Let Down from Heaven; *SGGK Sir Gawain and the Green Knight*; *WB* The Wife of Bath's Prologue and Tale (Chaucer).

INDEX 155

Kruger, Steven F., 124n7, 129n12, 140n34
kynodesme, 15, 16

Langland, William, *Piers Plowman*,
 79–80, 131n30, 135n75, 143n61
language, 6, 17, 19, 32–33, 45, 52, 72, 126n2
Lanser, Susan S., 115n23
law: Augustine, 24, 126n23; *BLF*, 38,
 39, 40, 46; Christ's fulfilment of, 16,
 62; Jewish, 17–18, 22, 119n37, 120n39,
 123n64; old/new dualism, 23, 27, 28, 31,
 38–40, 44, 84–85, 87, 130n16; Paul, 2, 16,
 20–23, 30, 123n64; Philo, 19; *PS*, 27, 28,
 29; *SGGK*, 66, 67, 68, 77; *WB*, 91–93
layers, 5, 19, 21, 25, 29, 32, 33, 35, 46, 95, 98
legalism, 78, 95, 97, 100, 134n68
Letter LXX (Jerome), 114n22
letter/spirit dualism: Augustine, 48; *BL*,
 35–36; Circumcision of Christ, 61–65;
 Hugh of Saint-Victor, 84, 137n10;
 marriage, 85–86; Paul, 1–2, 3, 8, 12–13,
 20, 21–22, 24, 31, 33, 38, 119n37, 123n63;
 PS, 28, 29; *SGGK*, 61, 65–67; textuality,
 35; *WB*, 95, 99, 138n25. *See also* literal/
 spiritual dualism
Leviticus, 14
Levy, Bernard S., 127n3
Life of Bruno (Ruotger), 113n15
lips, circumcised, 32, 48, 75, 78, 113n15,
 123n2, 124n3
Lipton, Sara, 142n47
literal/spiritual dualism: Ambrose,
 61–62; Augustine, 33, 35, 40; *BLF*, 45,
 47–48; Christ, 63, 130n16; Christians,
 46, 47–48; Circumcision of Christ,
 63; marriage, 85–86, 100; Paul, 1, 3, 9,
 18–24, 31, 54, 67, 119n37, 120n41, 121n45;
 PS, 29; *SGGK*, 74, 75, 76; uncircumcision, 89; *WB*, 89, 92–93, 95, 100, 102;
 "Wedding of Sir Gawain and Dame
 Ragnelle, The," 100. *See also* letter/
 spirit dualism
*Literal Meaning of Genesis in Twelve
 Books, The* (Augustine), 9, 32, 34–35,
 37, 43, 48, 124n7. *See also* Boy with the
 Long Foreskin (Augustine)

literalism, 46, 66, 78, 83, 89, 92–93, 95,
 142n47
literality, 139n25
literary act, circumcision as, 5, 8–10, 103
literary appropriation, 4
literary-theoretical concept, foreskin as,
 1–8, 19–27, 30–31, 106
liturgical calendar, 63–64
Loathly Lady, 64, 73, 92, 96–98, 101
Lochrie, Karma, 141n44
Lombard, Peter, 84–85
Love, Nicholas, *The Mirror of the Blessed
 Life of Jesus Christ*, 4, 112n10
loyalty, male, 56–58, 128n9
Luke's Gospel, 4–5
Luther, Martin, 3
Lydgate, John, 57

Maccabean Revolt, 16
Makarewicz, Mary Raynelda, 146n85
male/female distinction, 25, 26, 83,
 120n39, 140n34
male, masculine: body, 16, 26, 52–61, 66,
 67, 91, 100, 129n12; contradictory, 52,
 57–61, 66–67; female and, 25, 26, 83,
 95, 120n39, 140n34; interpretation, 6–7;
 loyalty, 56–58, 128n9; *SGGK*, 52, 56–61,
 71, 128nn9–10; textuality, 55, 59
male loyalty, 56–58, 128n9
Manicheans, 34
marital affection, 85, 137n18
marriage, 10, 72, 82–102, 136–38nn,
 143nn55,58–59, 144n65
Martial, 17, 117n14
Martin, Priscilla, 133n57
Marvin, William Perry, 132n40, 133n54
masculine textual body, 26, 52–61, 67
matrimony. *See* marriage
Matthew's Gospel, 78
McLaughlin, Megan, 142n47
McNamer, Sarah, 127n5
meaning: circumcision, 45; foreskin, 1–2,
 20–22; Paul, 123n64; *SGGK*, 64, 67,
 72–73, 74–75; words and, 2
medieval narrative, 1, 3
medieval narratology, 7, 114n23

Melville, Herman, *Moby-Dick*, 103
Menander, 114n22
metanarration, 28, 29, 41, 73–75, 122n60
metaphor, 2, 14, 106. *See also* allegory
Middle Platonism, 18
mind, 17–19, 48, 126n25
Minnis, Alistair, 145n84
Mirk, John, 127n3
*Mirror of the Blessed Life of Jesus Christ,
   The* (Love), 4, 112n10
Moby-Dick (Melville), 103
moderation, 15, 37, 124n9
modern circumcision, 105–8, 149n16,
   150n17
monarchy/democracy distinction, 104,
   148n8
monastics, 47–49, 75
Moses, 1, 14, 32, 86

nakedness, 65, 131n30
narration, extradiegetic, 28
narration, intradiegetic, 28
narrative: circumcision, 8–10, 13, 31, 33,
   45, 75; inner/outer dualism, 5, 33; medieval, 1, 3; reordering, 44–45; space,
   28–29, 122n59; time, 9, 27–28, 33, 36,
   41–45, 122n59, 125n17. *See also* allegorical narrative; circumcision, textual;
   circumlogical narrative
narrative, allegorical. *See* allegorical
   narrative
narrative, circumlogical. *See* circumlogical narrative
narrative body, 7, 29. *See also* body,
   textual
narrative excess, 78–80, 135nn75–76
narrative time, 9, 27–28, 33, 36, 41–45,
   122n59, 125n17
narratology, 7, 114n23
Nedham, Marchamont, 148n8
new/old dualism. *See* old/new dualism
New Testament, 12, 39, 46. *See also* Peter
   and the Sheet Let Down from Heaven;
   *names of individual New Testament
   books*
New Year's Day, 64–65, 76

New York Post, 150n17
Nightingale, Andrea, 124n3
Noah, 76, 131n29, 134n66
nominalization, 116n3
nothing, circumcision and uncircumcision as, 106
"nothing something," foreskin as, 48–49

Oakden, James Parker, 135n76
Odysseus, 57
Old English alliterative poetry, 79, 135n72
"old man," 44, 46, 102, 130n16
old/new dualism: *BLF*, 33, 36, 38–40, 46;
   Christ, 130n16; circumcision and, 23,
   33, 36, 85; law, 23, 27, 28, 31, 38–40, 44,
   84–85, 87, 130n16; Lombard, 84–85;
   marriage, 85, 137n18; Paul, 23, 44; *PS*,
   27, 28, 31; *SGGK*, 54–55; *WB*, 91, 92,
   96–97, 98, 100, 102, 145n79; "Wedding
   of Sir Gawain and Dame Ragnelle,
   The," 100
Old Testament: circumcision, 13, 14,
   21, 32, 46; foreskin, 13–14, 39, 44, 46;
   interpretation, 14, 34–35; New Testament and, 24, 44, 86, 126n23; repetition, 29–30; *SGGK*, 74, 81; *WB*, 91. *See
   also names of individual Old Testament
   books*
Olympic athletes, 15, 117n12
O'Malley, John W., 130n18
Origen, 24, 113n15, 118n26
Osberg, Richard, 135n72
outer/inner dualism. *See* inner/outer
   dualism
Owen, Charles A., Jr., 139n25

Pacatula, Letter to (Jerome), 82
pagan literature, 4, 33, 114n22, 125n20
Pancaro, Severino, 129n16
parallelisms, 71, 133n46
Pardoner's Tale (Chaucer), 90–91, 141n38,
   146n85
Passion, 62, 64
passions, 15, 18–19, 113n15
Patience, 133n57, 134n67
patrilineal history, 57–58, 59, 81

A. W. STROUSE is a poet and an adjunct professor of medieval literature, as well as the author of many scholarly articles, poems, and art projects.